The Business
of Coaching

The
Business
of
Coaching

A COMPREHENSIVE GUIDE
TO STARTING AND GROWING
YOUR COACHING PRACTICE

Dorcas Kelley

CLARITY IN ACTION
Salinas, California

Published by: Clarity In Action,
a division of Kelley-Naumchik Consulting L.L.C.
ISBN 0-9706086-2-4 (bookset)

The Business of Coaching℠ is a service mark
of Kelley-Naumchik Consulting L.L.C.

CLARITY IN ACTION
19250 Reavis Way
Salinas, California 93907-1352
(831) 663-5364
FAX: (831) 769-9035
EMAIL: info@clarityinaction.com

Visit our web sites: www.thebusinessofcoaching.com
and www.clarityinaction.com

10   9   8   7   6   5   4

Designed and composed by John Reinhardt Book Design

Printed in the United States of America.

For Chris — husband, friend, life and business partner — for hours of help and advice along with his unending support and love.

Acknowledgments

Thank you to the many coaches and colleagues who through emails, conversations, coaching sessions, teleclasses, presentations, and workshops have provided a wealth of questions, perspectives, feedback, stories, and ideas. This book is written for you, and is also shaped by you.

My sincerest thanks go to my brother-in-law Howard Daniel and my longtime friend Karin Carter for their editorial wisdom and expertise.

I lovingly acknowledge the impact that my late father — Dr. Robert L. Kelley (a professor and author) — has had on this book. My memories of him motivate me every day.

Contents

SECTION TWO
COVERING THE LEGAL BASES 39

*Help others achieve their dreams
and you will achieve yours.*

LES BROWN

SECTION THREE
FINANCIAL MATTERS   73

*Life is like playing a violin in public
and learning the instrument as one goes on.*

SAMUEL BUTLER

*Hard work spotlights the character of people:
some turn up their sleeves,
some turn up their noses,
and some don't turn up at all.*

SAM EWING

*Success is not the result of spontaneous
combustion. You must set yourself on fire.*

REGGIE LEACH

*I am always doing that which I can not do,
in order that I may learn how to do it.*

PABLO PICASSO

Introduction

*Real success is finding your lifework
in the work that you love.*

DAVID MCCULLOUGH

CONGRATULATIONS ON YOUR DECISION to be a personal and/or business coach, a rewarding and satisfying career! The profession of coaching is experiencing unprecedented growth and being a coach is not only a fulfilling experience, it can also be profitable.

I've found that the most successful coaches play three distinct roles within their businesses:

1. The insightful and compassionate coach who supports and challenges clients
2. The confident and enthusiastic marketer who enrolls and retains clients
3. The savvy entrepreneur who establishes and manages the coaching business

All three roles are needed and no one role is more important than the others. Being a gifted coach does not ensure that you are prepared to run a successful coaching practice. The business of coaching is just that — a business. Using your coaching skills of intuition, listening, and curiosity is just a portion of what is needed to make your business successful. Even if you only coach one person for a fee, you still have a coaching business, just a small one.

This book is focused on developing your entrepreneur and marketer roles. You'll find out how to start a coaching practice — from crafting your business vision and plan, to picking a company name, setting up your financial accounts, insuring your business, and paying taxes. You'll also learn how to manage and grow your business — from developing a marketing plan and marketing materials, to executing that plan and networking effectively. In addition, you will learn how to successfully transition to the world of self-employment and stay focused and organized.

Starting and growing a coaching business is both a "doing" and "being" adventure. There are tasks and activities to undertake (the "doing" aspect) and you may find yourself wondering if you are doing them correctly or if you are missing something. If you are concerned about this, stop, relax, and take a deep breath. This book and the companion workbook will walk you through all of the steps.

One of my objectives in creating this book is not just to assemble and impart this information to you, but to help you realize that establishing, managing, and marketing your business need not be complex, confusing, intimidating, or burdensome. It's not rocket science! The activities themselves are not difficult, and nearly all the information you need can be found in this book and the companion workbook.

My second objective is to explicitly address the "being" aspect of your business, a topic that is typically overlooked by many small-business start-up books. How you "be" in your business — how you think of yourself, your business, your purpose in the world, how your thoughts translate into action and behavior — will have a powerful impact on your success. In fact, it is a key driver of your success. I'm going to point out how your thoughts and perceptions can facilitate (or hinder) your business success.

My third objective comes from my passionate commitment to the coaching industry. Our industry will only be as strong and successful as the individual coaches within it. If we all have professional, ethical, profitable, and successful businesses then that will be the standard for the industry. Wouldn't that be great? If, instead, we do not provide excellent service to our clients, have dubious ethics, and manage our affairs and our businesses in an unprofessional manner, then our industry is doomed to failure. I want us *all* to be wildly successful coaches, and for the power of coaching to reach the entire world. Together, we can achieve this vision.

I've written this book for both the novice and the established coach. Once you've read this book, none of the topics covered will remain a mystery to you. Furthermore, the workbook contains activities that cover each of the chapter topics as well as additional resources (print and web based) to assist your continued learning. You will find this bookset to be a valuable resource for your business library, and by the end of this book you will be managing and marketing your business with confidence and enthusiasm.

How This Book Is Organized

I recommend that you read through the book in order, completing the associated activities in The Business of Coaching Workbook as you go. For each chapter in this book, there is a corresponding chapter in the workbook which contains action steps, charts, inquiries, and resources for nearly all of the topics in the chapter text. In this way you will learn the information for each business element and will then apply what you learned in the workbook. Even if you have an aversion to workbooks, please check this one out. I think you'll be pleasantly surprised.

The book is organized in a logical sequence, starting with

you and your business vision, then traveling into the worlds of legal, financial, marketing, and day-to-day operations. Enjoy the journey!

In **Section One**, the focus is on you — your business vision, how you see yourself as the leader of your business, and your business plan. In addition, we'll cover my "Recipe For Business Success" which provides a big-picture overview of the business start-up and growth process. These topics work together to provide the foundation for your business.

Section Two ventures into the world of business legal issues, such as legal structures, business and personal insurance, and local and state requirements.

The financial elements are addressed in **Section Three**, including budgeting, record keeping, financial accounts, invoicing, taxes, and saving for retirement.

Section Four is focused on your marketing role: developing a marketing plan and a brand identity, naming your business, creating marketing materials, marketing activities, as well as developing effective networking skills.

Section Five covers topics focused within the four walls of your office: transitioning to self-employment, staying focused and organized, addressing procrastination, setting up your business contact methods (e.g., phone, fax, email), handling paperwork, and selecting appropriate office equipment.

Laying
the Foundation

*The beginning is the most important
part of the work.*

PLATO

JUST AS A BUILDING CONTRACTOR will lay the foundation before the walls are constructed, so too will you need to build the foundation for your business before you focus on supporting activities such as legal, finances, marketing, and day-to-day operations.

What is the foundation for a business? In a word — you. You are the foundation for your business. Who you are, how you see the world, your uniqueness, values, and experiences are the concrete and girders that shape and support your business. Throughout the book we will continue to explore various aspects of you, and this journey begins now.

In this section we'll start off with a big picture overview of the business start-up process, then explore the vision you hold for your business, and the plans that spring from that vision. We'll also discuss your feelings about being a business owner, and how to fully embrace that role.

So open your mind, throw out your assumptions, quiet your gremlins, and let's begin!

1

Your Recipe for Business Success

*To accomplish great things we must first dream,
then visualize, then plan . . . believe . . . act!*

ALFRED A. MONTAPERT

D ID YOU KNOW that over half of all new businesses fail within four years? This startling statistic comes from a U.S. Small Business Administration study that found that only 44% of the businesses started in 1992 were still around in 1996[1]. That means that in just four short years over half of these new businesses (56%) had closed their doors forever. Often the dreams and aspirations of the business owner die along with the company, despite untold hours of diligent effort.

My goal is to increase the rate of small business success, one business at a time, starting with *your* business!

I know from my own experience that starting a business can seem complex and confusing, but it doesn't need to be. It can be the most fun, challenging, creative, and rewarding job you've ever had.

---

[1] Dr. Richard Boden, Jr., "Establishment Employment Change and Survival, 1992-1996," Small Business Research Summary, U.S. Small Business Administration, Office of Advocacy , No. 200, September 2000.

When I first started my business, I was concerned that managing it would be time-consuming and arduous. I was relieved to learn that it's neither rocket science nor the huge burden I had imagined. I also found that, as a result of spending some time and energy to create a strong foundation for my business, I felt more competent and confident in my own skills and in my role as business owner and coach.

Since you're reading this book, I'm anticipating that you are ready to invest some energy and time in making your own business successful, and I'm glad! In this book I hope to cover nearly all the tasks, information, and processes you will need to grow your own successful coaching business.

But first I want to give you the big picture of this process, so that you can see the context for the details I'll provide later. Since I love to cook (and eat!), many of my metaphors are related to cooking. The metaphor I use for starting and growing a business is that of a recipe — various ingredients are needed to make a tasty dish and each ingredient is indispensable to success.

Before We Start Cooking

There are three important things you need to know about the ingredients:

1. All the ingredients, or aspects of your business, are equally important and need to be in the recipe in some form. You don't get to pick and choose which ones you want to include and ignore the rest — not if you want your business to be healthy and successful!

2. In addition, they will all remain essential throughout the life of your business, and will require your continued attention. In a way, businesses are like houses — they both need periodic attention and maintenance; otherwise they fall apart. The ingredients are not one-

time events but rather ongoing activities.

3. The good news is that nothing is permanent. Each of the ingredients will change over time. In fact this is one of the most wonderful characteristics of running a business — it never sits still, never stays the same! Your clients, the market, your interests or areas of focus might change. This is to be expected, not avoided. Your first, second, and even third pass through these nine aspects will not lock you in, nor do you have to wait until your decision or work is perfectly right before you can take action. When change is expected and even looked for, the concepts of "perfect" and "right" become meaningless. The life of your business is a process, just as your own life is a process; your business will change over time, just as we all change over time. Expect the changes and welcome them. With each change, take time to determine which aspects of your business are impacted, and adjust accordingly.

The Ingredients

Like a cook, let me start by setting out the nine ingredients called for in your recipe for business success. We'll slice 'em and dice 'em — explain them — in greater detail just below and, again, in subsequent chapters.

1. Business Vision
2. Empowerment
3. Coach Training and Experience
4. Business Plan
- You as a Coach
- Legal Foundation
- Financial Foundation
- Marketing Plan and Activities
- Day-to-Day Operations

Wondering why I've numbered some of the ingredients but not others? Because in this recipe, the first four items are the starting points; they provide the foundation for the remaining items, which can be addressed in almost any order (though I've found that the order listed is the most effective).

Business Vision

Going back to the recipe metaphor, you can think of your business vision as the flame that's cooking it all up. Your business vision provides the heat; it is the starting point for your business — your dream, passion, aspiration, and hope for your work in the world. Your vision will feed into every other aspect of your business, and that's why it's important to work on this step first.

You as an Empowered Business Owner

For your business to be successful, you need to treat your business as a *business,* not a hobby or something you do on the side. You also need to see yourself as a business owner as well as a coach. You are the person in charge of your business! After all, if it's not you, who is it? Another part of being empowered is knowing your value and setting your fees accordingly.

Coach Training and Experience

This ingredient is focused on the specific coaching skills and expertise you bring to your work, through your formal coach training and through your client work.

There is a growing number of coaching schools, established to help you learn and apply specific coaching skills. The International Coach Federation, which describes itself as "the professional association of personal and business coaches that seeks to preserve the integrity of coaching around the globe," has accredited some of these schools.

There is wide variety in the characteristics of the schools.

Recipe for Business Success

Your Business Vision

Day-to-Day Operations
Marketing Plan and Activities
Financial Foundation
Legal Foundation

You as a Coach
Business Plan
Coach Training and Experience

You As An Empowered
Business Owner

For example, some schools offer weekly course sessions spread across several months, others offer intensive courses lasting only a few days. Instruction ranges from totally in-person to totally virtual. No one way is better than another, though there may be a few characteristics that are the best choices for you individually.

Each characteristic involves a trade-off, for example in-person connection and learning vs. travel costs, or potentially slower-paced learning vs. intense immersion. Only you can determine which combination of characteristics will best fit your needs and your learning style.

SELECTING A SCHOOL

How to choose between the schools? Here are some factors to consider when making your decision.

- How do you learn best? What is your own natural learning style? No offense intended, but the typical adult learns best in a monkey see — monkey do style, which would include demonstrations of coaching skills, followed by discussion and practice, lots of practice!
- Look at the location of the schools. Which ones offer an instructional framework that fits your own style and requires the least travel? (Unless you want to travel!)
- Look at the scheduling — what works best for you?
- Is the school ICF-accredited? This is one indication of the maturity and comprehensiveness of the curriculum. Keep in mind that there are always schools in the process of being accredited, so make sure to ask whether your desired school, if not currently accredited, is in the process or has plans to become ICF-accredited.
- Talk to graduates of the school. Each school should have a list of graduates you can contact. What are their impressions? What did they see as the pros and cons of the school? Are they successful coaches? What is their coaching style? Is it a style you feel comfortable with? How

did they make their decision?

- Cost and payment plans. Although cost is typically a significant factor in this decision, please try to keep it in perspective. If you are hoping that coaching will become a viable career, then your coaching education is an investment in that career. So include cost as part of the decision, but remember that it is only one criterion. Most mature schools are roughly similar in their pricing structure — although they vary in pricing, they are all within a range. Also, most schools offer plans that let you spread payments out over time.

- Some coaching schools offer a certification program as well as skills training courses. In addition, you can apply for certification from the ICF once you have accumulated enough client coaching hours. Certification is more than just letters after your name! A solid certification program will not only provide you with a differentiating characteristic that is helpful in your marketing, it should also deepen and strengthen your expertise in the field.

- Schools may also specialize in a specific type of coaching, or coaching niche. For example, a school may be geared toward therapists, or focused solely on corporate coaching. If you know what coaching specialty you want to pursue, this would be a characteristic of interest to you.

- What type of business-related support or training does the school offer? You are embarking on a journey to become a coach and an entrepreneur/small business owner. Does the school offer an adequate range of courses and other resources to help in this area?

- Lastly, remember that coaching is an interactive, relationship-based profession, and look for a school that will maximize interaction and the development of relationship and communication skills. As adults, we typically do not learn effectively just by reading or listening. We need interaction, practice, and person-to-person support to make our learning experiences stick. To increase your chances for success, a program with a highly interactive, personal, and application-oriented format is the optimal choice.

COACHING EXPERIENCE

Once you've started a training program, your focus will shift to accumulating coaching experience. Eventually, it is important to focus on a specific niche (more about that in Chapter Eleven), but in your first year, try to coach as many different people as possible. Whether you call them practice clients or pro-bono clients is unimportant. What is important is to accumulate as much actual coaching experience as possible. Just as with any new skill, the way to improve and learn is through practice … practice … practice! Ask your friends, family, colleagues, neighbors, mail carrier, anyone! Also, if you have a favorite nonprofit organization, offer them free coaching — you'll feel good because you'll be helping a worthwhile organization, you'll get the organization's name on your client list, and they'll benefit from your coaching. It's a win-win!

However you do it, it's important to gain experience. You will learn so much more when you put the skills training into action right away. Be ready to experiment with new coaching skills and techniques. Typically, what differentiates a master coach from a novice is the master's ability to adapt coaching methods for optimal results. This adaptability comes solely from experience.

This ingredient — coach training and experience — is highly personalized and unique to your needs, your life, and your goals. Therefore, we won't be discussing it further in this book. However, for further information on ICF-accredited coaching schools, please visit their website at www.coachfederation.org.

Business Plan

A business plan is like a roadmap. Would you leave on a car trip from San Francisco to New York without a roadmap? Probably not. Even if you basically know the way, a map keeps you from getting sidetracked or wandering aimlessly. It also helps you keep track of the progress you've made and how far you have left to go.

You as a Coach

As coaches, we help our clients define and pursue a fulfilling and successful life, however they envision it. We also need to walk the talk, meaning that we need to define and pursue our own fulfilling and successful lives. Just as we help clients become more focused and purposeful, we should do the same for ourselves.

To return to the metaphor, it means we need to eat our own cooking — that we not just talk about pursuing a more fulfilling life, but also take action to make it a reality. I don't mean to imply that coaches need to be better or more together than our clients. After all, we are just humans: imperfect, flawed, learning, and growing. But we need to be aware of our selves, our lives, our impact on the world, our goals, and our progress. We want to be receptive clients for the coaching that life brings *us!* As people, and as coaches, we will be growing and changing all the time. These changes might come through our life experiences and the wisdom they bring, through formal self-discovery and self-development, and through work with our own coaches.

Don't lose sight of your responsibility to define and pursue your own goals, just as you help your clients pursue theirs. This is one reason why it's important to have your own coach. I know I couldn't have accomplished a fraction of what I've done without my coaches. They have helped me define and achieve my own evolving and fulfilling life!

Because this ingredient is so specific to your life and your dreams, we won't be addressing it any further in this book. However, this is a great topic to address with your own coach.

Legal Foundation

Your business's legal foundation is a relatively small, but very important ingredient. Small both in the number of tasks and in the relative amount of time they will take. But important in the implications these tasks have for your business.

Parts of the legal foundation will come from your local and state or provincial governments, and a few will come from the federal or country level. No book can include all the details for each requirement since they vary by city, county, state, province and country. So you will need to supply some of your own time to investigate the specifics for your location. However, we'll cover the basic concepts and point you in the right direction.

Financial Foundation

Just as finances play an important role in your personal life, so too do they play a key role in your business life. There are many components of a strong financial foundation, some as mundane and straightforward as setting up a checking account, others as complex as business taxes and saving for retirement.

Many coaches avoid the whole area of finances, preferring to be blissfully ignorant. Unfortunately, blissful ignorance is typically short-lived, and the resulting lack of adequate financial planning is the major cause of business failure. But don't panic, you don't have to be a CPA to run a business! Most of the financial tasks are quite simple and there are lots of professionals who will be happy to work with you on the more complex portions, for a well-earned fee.

Even if you choose to hire a professional to handle some of the more complex aspects, you should still have a general understanding of them so that you can be a savvy consumer and an intelligent client. This principle is already in practice in your personal life — you may not be an auto mechanic, but you know, in general, how an automobile works. If a mechanic tried to sell you a new set of tires to repair an over-heating engine, you know enough to question the recommendation.

Some aspects of your financial foundation, such as your budget, can be done only by you. Luckily (and contrary to what you might think) the process of budgeting is not lengthy; a budget takes only a few hours to create and maintain, and it will have a long-lasting positive impact on your business. Your budget sets the foundation for your marketing plan by helping you create some measurable financial goals for your business such as how much money you want to make in the next six to nine months, as well as how much you want to spend during that time. Don't be frightened. Finances are your friend!

Marketing Plan and Activities

Ah, yes, marketing. Why, you might ask, isn't marketing listed first or second on the list of ingredients, something to be done sooner rather than later? Isn't marketing what it's all about? Yes, it's true that marketing is how we get our clients, so it certainly is a very important task.

However, many coaches fall into the trap of thinking that it is the *only* task and that if one does marketing well everything else will fall into place. Alas, this is a fallacy. Remember that each of the nine ingredients is equally important, and that marketing is just one of them. There is much more to your business than just marketing. It is a critical ingredient, to be sure, but without a business plan, or adequate coach training, or a legal foundation, or financial targets, marketing won't be successful. Your marketing will be much more effective, and efficient, with the other elements in place.

The topic of marketing is very broad, and in general it can be broken into two main subtopics: strategy/planning and execution/activities. One without the other is not effective.

You may have the best marketing plan in the world, but without action, you won't have much success. Conversely, if all you have is action, with no plan or strategy, you will find yourself very busy, very tired, and very discouraged. Therefore, we will address both areas.

Day-to-Day Operations

What days and hours will you work? When and how will you handle your invoicing? When will you have client appointments? What equipment will your office have? How will you manage your time effectively? How will you manage the paperwork? What will you do if you notice that you are procrastinating on an important task? How many phone lines will you need? What Internet service provider will you use? All these questions are part of this topic. It is the tactical structure of your work, and you may be surprised by the power of this ingredient.

Remember that 56% of businesses fail within their first four years? Lack of adequate financial planning was already mentioned as a main cause of failure. Another major cause is a lack of skills and processes in the areas of time management and organization.

We all have only 24 hours in each day, and 7 days in each week. There is no way around this constraint. The efficient use of time is critical to your success, and the equipment you use, the schedules you follow, and the techniques and processes you employ in your business directly impact it.

Let's start cooking! Bon Appétit!

2

Crafting Your Business Vision

Whatever you can do or dream you can, begin it.
Boldness has genius, magic and power in it.
Begin it now.

GOETHE

D O YOU HAVE A VISION FOR YOUR LIFE? An idea of what you want it to look like or feel like? I bet you do.

A vision, or you might call it a dream or longing, is a very powerful thing. It can motivate us to action, steer our decisions and priorities, and help us follow our progress. Our most passionate goals all spring from a vision. Just as we benefit from having a vision for our lives, so too do we benefit from having a vision for our businesses.

Don't confuse a business vision with a business plan. Your business vision is a picture — the *big* picture view of your business, your dream, your image of how you want your business to look and feel. It is filled with emotion and passion. In contrast, a business plan is a roadmap — more tactical, more measurable, more action-oriented, a way to bring your vision closer to reality. We'll talk more about business plans in Chapter Four.

Your coaching business is not something wholly separate

from you — it's a vital aspect of your life and your life's work. Being a coach is both who you are and what you do. Your coaching business is the vehicle by which you bring your passion and your coaching gifts to the world. It is the formal structure that connects you as a coach with the rest of the world. Clearly this is a critical aspect of your life, and it deserves a strong vision to shape, guide, and support it.

A Vision's Purpose

So what is the purpose of a business vision? At a high level, it is to articulate or describe your dream, to put you in touch with the passions and emotions and desires that drew you to this profession. By acknowledging your vision, and by consciously thinking about it and describing it, you will receive two major benefits.

The first is that your vision will become clearer and better defined, and therefore a step closer to reality. Just as you help your clients define what a more fulfilling life would look like for them, the process of crafting a business vision asks you to define what a fulfilling life would look like for your business. What is the bigger game your business will play in the world?

As you have probably experienced with your clients, just the act of defining a vision helps them move toward that goal. It also helps them recognize aspects of the vision when they appear in their lives. This is a deceptively simple but critical outcome of this step — how will you know that you're moving toward your business vision if you haven't clearly articulated what it will look, feel, and be like?

On a related note, if you have developed a personal life vision, I recommend that you take time to weave it together with your business vision. They have big areas of overlap and must work together to support and enhance each other.

The second big benefit of crafting your business vision is that it will give you the motivation, energy, and commitment to get through activities or times that aren't fun or rewarding. For example, I have a client whose business vision includes providing medical services to poverty-level children to increase their chances of a successful, healthy life. The clarity and passion behind this vision has kept her motivated during her years in medical school, despite the strenuous workload and the low-income student lifestyle.

Your business vision can provide the same benefit to you: help you stay motivated, passionate, goal-oriented, and committed to your dream. So in those times when you are doing more marketing than generating revenue, what might feel like more work than pleasure, when you are paying business taxes or managing your finances, you'll be able to focus on how these mundane activities move you closer to bringing your vision to life.

Without a compelling business vision, "work" steps and activities can seem hollow and uninviting. Your business vision will provide you with the fuel to get you started and keep you in motion; the work will flow more easily.

Please don't confuse vision with goals. A goal might be "I want to have a flexible schedule." You may feel very passionate about this, but it isn't a vision, it's a goal, a state that you want to get to. Visions don't have a final destination, because they are constantly unfolding. You can't achieve a vision, but you can achieve a goal. See the difference? Both are vital and they work hand-in-hand! The key is to harness your passion in order to move toward your vision and to reach your goals.

It's important to know that a business vision can take a bit of time to coalesce, so please don't think that you can sit down and hammer one out. Don't feel frustrated if your vision comes to you in bits and pieces. Let it develop slowly; daydream and see what comes to you. Keep a journal about your business vision so you can review its evolution.

Also be aware that your vision will change over time — just as your business will change and you will change. It's all a work in progress — just like life. So don't be surprised when a new element of your vision emerges weeks, months, or even years down the line. Be curious about this new element: what does it bring you? If you choose to incorporate it into your vision, review the other elements to ensure that the entire vision remains cohesive and alive as ever.

Your business vision is only for you; it's not for clients, colleagues or marketing materials. You may choose to talk about your business vision with others, but its purpose is for you alone. So develop a vision that speaks to you and gets you fired up to make it real. At the same time, don't be upset or surprised if the business vision that you feel really committed to leaves others feeling ho-hum. Remember, it's *your* vision, not theirs. It's wonderful if others get caught up in the passion of your vision, but it's not required.

Dig Deeper to Turn Up the Passion

If you find yourself with a vision that is interesting and intriguing, but is not yet really exciting, here's a way to turn up the passion. Visions often get juicier as you dig deeper, asking yourself a series of "whys?" or "because of…." or "in service of…" questions to uncover the next layer. To illustrate, I'll describe the evolution of my own business vision.

When I started my coaching business, I knew I wanted to work with businesses, which is logical given my years of business and management consulting experience. (More about niches in Chapter Eleven.) I felt a desire to work with small business owners in particular because I wanted them, and their businesses, to succeed and I knew that coaching can help make that happen. So far I've uncovered four characteristics of my business vision: small businesses, small business owners, having a positive impact on the business, and the desire for their success. This is an example of an intriguing business vision, but one that doesn't stir much passion. So let's dig deeper.

Why did I want to have an impact on small businesses? In service of what? Why does the success of small businesses matter to me? To the world? As I dug deeper, I found that my vision addressed two distinct levels: an individual picture and a bigger picture.

On the individual level — the level of the specific small business owner — I realized that I wanted to work with people like them because they have an extremely challenging time trying to balance their personal and their business lives. A small business owner often eats, breathes, and lives for her business, and this can have a disastrous impact on personal and inner lives. Running your own business, whether you have zero, 50, or 100 employees is far more complex and consuming than a typical corporate job, even at the CEO level. Small business owners wear many hats, serving as strategist and visionary as well as implementer, plus everything else in between. So the concept of balance takes on a whole new level of meaning — balancing work and personal life as well as balancing the multiple roles within the business. Clearly, small business owners can benefit enormously from coaching.

In addition, still on the individual level, I saw how my consulting experience and business expertise would be of great service to the health of the business, which would facilitate the owner's peace of mind and free up energy to focus on establishing a more positive balance in her life. The business owner would be in a better position to achieve success in both her work and personal life. Happy owner, happy company, happy coach. I start to feel more energy when I describe this part of my vision — can you feel it?

The other level — the bigger picture — adds even more juice to the vision. Why do I care if the owner is successful in life and work? Other than the fact that all humans deserve a happy and fulfilling life, there must be another reason. Let's dig deeper into this second level and find out.

I realized that one of the reasons I am so passionate about small businesses is that they are the economic engine of our country. Every big corporation started out as a small business. Think about any big company, and it probably started as just an idea in someone's head — Microsoft with Bill Gates and Paul Allen, Hewlett-Packard Company with Bill Hewlett and Dave Packard. They started as small businesses, not knowing if they would succeed or fail.

Our economy is a financial ecosystem — there is a wide variety of types and shapes and sizes of businesses. Some grow into big corporations, others stay small, and still others die off. But each plays an important role in the ecosystem, which could not survive without all its component business "organisms." Each business plays a vital role in the economy, just as the ant and the elephant — and all other creatures — do in the natural world.

So part of my vision includes helping to strengthen a vital aspect of our economy, increasing the success of the small business sector, one business at a time. Not only will I be helping the individual business owner, I'll also be impacting the whole economy. How cool is that?!

This vision, with its multiple levels of positive impact and service, keeps me motivated to get going and learn new things every day. I may not enjoy every moment, but I know that each task is moving me toward my vision.

Can you feel the energy in that vision now? I can! Notice that I arrived at this juicy place by continuing to ask (and answer) "why?" or "what is this in service of?" to expose another layer of my business vision. By digging deeper and deeper, I discover new wells of motivation and excitement.

Don't feel bad if my business vision doesn't stir the passion inside of you — that's not important. It's meant to stir the passion inside *me*. You will talk with other coaches and may not be enraptured by their business visions either. That's OK! The objective of your business vision is to get *you* enraptured. That's why I mentioned earlier that a business vision is for you alone, to get you fired up and excited. Your business vision might be of interest to others, but don't judge its quality and rightness based on how excited others get. The focus is on how excited it makes *you*!

The Quest for "Right"

Speaking of rightness, our western culture puts a big emphasis on getting things "right" or "perfect." We grow up wanting to go to the right school and get the right degree to get the right job with the right company in the right location, marry the right person and settle down in the right house with the right number of kids. Whew! That's exhausting just to think about, let alone accomplish.

While working on your business vision, please set aside any expectations you may have about having to define the "right" or "perfect" vision. Since you already know that your business vision will change over time, the concepts of right and perfect lose their meaning. If you accept that your vision is a work in progress, then there is no right or wrong. Is your vision more right than mine? Is it more right than the vision you might have two years from now? Hopefully you see that these questions are just nonsensical.

I point this out because many new entrepreneurs get stuck in the "It's got to be perfect" place, and this quest for perfection is an exercise destined for frustration and failure because perfect doesn't exist!

This doesn't mean that you can just throw together a vision without much thought or effort. In fact, the opposite is true: good visions take time and effort to think about and document. Notice that I use the word "good" — not "right" or "perfect." The essential thing is that your vision speaks to you about what you want to accomplish, that it motivates you to stay on your chosen path, and gets you excited about your work, your learning, and your life.

I strongly suggest that you document your business vision in some fashion, for five main reasons.

- The act of documenting it will really sink the vision into your heart and soul (and memory).
- It will help you further expand and develop the vision.
- The documentation will be useful in the future, when you review your vision to get a burst of motivation, or as new aspects of your vision emerge in your work.
- Your business vision is a key input into your marketing plan and your brand. Documenting it will save you time and effort when you reach those activities.
- The documentation of your vision will be very useful when you have a significant decision to make. By re-immersing yourself in your vision, the optimal choice will become clearer. Your business vision will act like a touchstone, a reminder of your direction and purpose.

There is no right format for this documentation. You could write out your vision by hand or on a computer or with a crayon, in free form text or a poem or a sonnet. You could paint it or draw it, create a collage or compose a piece of music, sing it or speak it onto a tape or a CD. The key is to capture the thoughts, images, motivations, desires, passion, and emotions so that you can easily step back into your vision at any time and plug into its power.

One suggestion is to write a vision story. Imagine yourself 5, 8, or 10 years in the future, when your current vision has been achieved. You are reflecting back on the years, what you've accomplished, the path you took, the challenges and triumphs, the changes you have brought to your world. Write your vision story from that perspective and share your excitement and passion.

In Chapter Two of the workbook you'll find several pages of questions and exercises that will help you define, expand, and document your own compelling business vision.

3

Being an Empowered Business Owner

*Human beings, by changing the inner attitudes
of their minds, can change the outer aspects
of their lives.*

WILLIAM JAMES

WHY IS THIS TOPIC IMPORTANT ENOUGH that it has its own chapter? If you are running your own business, then you are a business owner. End of topic, right? But not all business owners see themselves as such. Do *you* think of yourself as a business owner? Going a step further, do you see yourself as the *CEO* of your business? You are!

The Power of Our Thoughts

As coaches, we are well acquainted with the powerful impact of how we view ourselves. If a client sees herself as small and insignificant, it's very likely that's how she talks, behaves, and is therefore seen by others. Our thoughts have tremendous impact not only on what we say, but also on our behavior, and the way others perceive and treat us.

So if you are running your own business, but don't think of yourself as a business owner (and perhaps even avoid the idea), what do you think the impact might be?

This ingredient — being an empowered business owner — is critical for your business success, because how you think of your business and your role in it often becomes reality. To have a successful business, you need to see and treat it as a true business, not as a hobby or something you do on the side. If you think of your coaching business as a hobby then that is what you'll have! That's not a bad thing, if it's what you want. But if it's not, then that way of thinking is an obstacle to success.

It doesn't matter that you are a one-person business — it is still a business. In 1995, there were over 3 million businesses in the U.S. with four or fewer people. Each of them was a real business.

Collapsing Success and Greed

When talking to coaches about this topic, I've noticed a tendency to collapse together different concepts. For example, seeing your coaching practice as a business and wanting it to be successful does not mean you have to become a greedy, hard-edged, workaholic focused only on the financial bottom line. As a coach, your life's work revolves around furthering human development and fulfillment. Wanting a successful business doesn't change that commitment.

Remember that even the world's best non-profit organizations — totally dedicated to helping others — are still businesses. Contrary to popular belief, the term "non-profit" does *not* mean the organization can't make a profit, only that any profit gets invested back into the organization. Well-known non-profits, such as the Girl Scouts, Red Cross, United Way, the Public Broadcasting Service (PBS), are noteworthy because they have had a significant positive impact on our society and because they are so long-lived. In turn, both of these characteristics have been made possible by the fact that these organizations see themselves as businesses, as well as mission-driven organizations.

I'm not suggesting that your business will be non-profit, just pointing out that it is not only possible, but also desirable, to develop a successful, profitable business and still be loving, compassionate, humanistic, and dedicated to the fulfillment of others. These are not mutually exclusive goals.

To achieve these goals, not only must you recognize your business as a business, but you must also think of yourself as a business owner and not just as a coach. You are the person in charge of your business. You are the CEO! After all, if not you, then who? *Someone* has to be in charge, and that someone is *you.*

It may be challenging to think of yourself as a CEO. Actually I use the term because it is often a big stretch to step into that role. But, let's face it, your business does have a CEO, and *you're it.*

CEO Images and Stories

Part of the challenge in accepting this role has to do with the image of CEOs in our culture. From the headlines to the comics page we see little but horror stories or negative stereotypes. They are often portrayed as ruthless men with dubious ethics and morals. Dilbert™ and Blondie™ don't offer much relief. Who'd want to sign up for the role of villain or buffoon?

I challenge you to look at the assumptions, stories, and myths in your head about what it means to be a CEO. What *you'd* have to be like to step into that role.

When I first thought about myself as a CEO, the image that came to mind was of a pompous, conservative, balding white male, with goofy glasses and an ill-fitting gray pinstripe suit. Yuck! I didn't want to be *that!* Yet it took me months to become conscious of that image and the assumptions that went with it. Meanwhile, I avoided claiming my CEO/business owner/entrepreneur role because of that image, acting as if I'd somehow become that unpleasant person just by seeing myself in the role! Once I recognized the absurdity of my fears, then I could finally embrace, explore, and enjoy the fact that I *am* the CEO of my business.

So what CEO images do you have in *your* head? What assumptions have you made up? When you hear the term CEO, what feelings and thoughts come up? In all likelihood, most of those assumptions, stories, images, and gremlins serve you very poorly! In fact, they will keep you confined and playing small in your business, and will stop you from fully assuming your role as CEO and business owner.

If those negative images and assumptions aren't true, then what is the truth about CEOs and business owners? One truth is that CEOs and business owners are as varied as the human race. They come in all shapes, sizes, temperaments, and levels of intelligence. There is no one way or right way to be a CEO and business owner. Or, perhaps it would be more accurate to say that you have your own unique and individual right way, the way that reflects who you are, your values, strengths, and interests. So toss out your old stories and make up new ones that work for you, reflecting who you are and your own style. What kind of CEO do *you* want to be?

Designing Your Unique CEO

Typically, CEO stands for Chief Executive Officer. But, it doesn't have to! Not only can you decide how you want to be as CEO, you can also determine what you want the acronym CEO to stand for in *your* business. You may want to be Chief Encouragement Officer or Chief Evolution Officer.

I have created several new definitions that I use when appropriate. For me, sometimes CEO means Creatively Evoking Options, because that's what I do with my clients. Other times it means Celebrate Every Obstacle because that's a very empowering perspective. You can determine how you want to act as CEO, and creating your own definitions is a great way to help do it. In fact, you can make a whole list of definitions and then use them as needed! I've found that this exercise has really helped me dispel the negative images I had of the term CEO and make it a playful, creative, empowered role I now eagerly embrace.

You'll find additional exercises in the workbook to help you define and step into your own unique CEO role.

Knowing Your Value

Part of embracing your role as CEO and business owner is establishing a fee structure that honors you and the value you bring to your clients. You have skills that help your clients achieve a more fulfilling life, and you have worked hard to build your coaching expertise.

You might think that the topic of fees should be included in the chapter on finances (and there is a small section), but I've found that fees are more an emotional and psychological issue than a mathematical one. The entire topic of fees — establishing them, talking about them, asking for them — can send any coach into a gremlin-filled tailspin. That's why I'm including this topic here and I ask that you stay in your empowered CEO perspective while reading this section.

As with many aspects of your business, there is no "right" answer when it comes to establishing your fee structure. You need to determine what feels best for you, for your current level of experience, and for your niche. Here are some considerations to ponder.

You've paid money and spent time and effort to be professionally trained as a coach, much as you might be trained in any other profession. Think about other professionals you interact with — accountants, lawyers, therapists, consultants,

medical professionals, auto mechanics, beauticians, financial advisors, massage therapists, carpenters, teachers, dog
trainers, just to name a few. All of them charge money for
their services, and you, as a consumer, are able to decide:
"Do I want to pay this much for this service?" Sometimes
yes, sometimes no, but you don't expect them to work for
free.

Several years ago, the ICF did a study that found that
trained coaches charge, on average, $200 a month for two
hours of coaching. These charges range from $100 to $600
or more a month, depending on the niche, skill level, and
type of coaching provided (for example personal, business,
or executive).

It's a common practice to charge less while in training and
as you ramp up your coaching skills. Your fee structure will
change over time as your expertise and reputation grow. My
first clients paid me $10 a session and I increased my fees as
I completed my training and gained experience.

You may also choose to have different fee structures for
different types of clients. I have one fee structure for my non-
profit clients, another for my private clients, and a third for
my corporate clients. Each type of client represents a different market, so the fees are adjusted accordingly.

Talking about fees is like talking about sex. It's awkward at
first and a bit embarrassing. Unless you've been self-employed
for years, you probably don't have much experience talking
about fees. So expect that it will be awkward and know that
the way to feel more comfortable is practice ... practice ...
practice!

Don't let your gremlins or your fears determine your fee
structure or keep you in a timid place. Keep your CEO hat
firmly on your head when you determine your fees and talk
about them with clients. It will get easier, I promise!

Creating Your Business Plan

All who have accomplished great things have had a great aim, have fixed their gaze on a goal which was high, one which sometimes seemed impossible.

ORISON SWETT MARDEN

I COMMEND YOUR BRAVERY! You've started reading this chapter even though the dreaded words "business plan" are in the title. Many new entrepreneurs will turn pale, gasp, and flee when hearing that phrase.

To reward your courage, I'd like to let you in on a secret — business plans do *not* need to be long, detailed, arduous, multi-sectioned, complex documents. So please throw out any assumptions you might have about what a business plan has to look like. It only has to look like something that will help you plan for your business success, stay motivated and on track toward your business goals.

Actually, to be more accurate, there are two main types of business plans. One is used to get loans or financing from sources such as banks or venture capitalists. This type of business plan does need to contain a fair amount of detailed information and it is the format that is typically thought of when speaking of a business plan. However, for the purposes of this book, the assumption is that you are not going to be taking your business plan to a bank or venture capitalist for start-up funding. One of the beauties of the coaching profession is that start-up expenses are relatively small, so there is rarely a need for outside funding.

The second type of business plan, and the one that is discussed in this book, is only for your use. It does not need lots of detailed tables or graphs or research, only enough to provide you with a roadmap for your business, including your plans and strategies, goals and milestones, as well as information regarding your target market.

Purpose of a Business Plan

What is the purpose of a business plan? In a nutshell, it serves to document your plans and goals moving you toward your business vision and to facilitate and track progress toward them. Sounds useful, yes?

Although there is no magic formula to guarantee business success, it's an article of faith that "A business owner who fails to plan, plans to fail." A business plan will help you think through your plans and strategies, define goals and measures of your success, help focus your time and energy, and recognize your achievements as well as your limitations. A business plan will act as a roadmap to direct you from where you are now to your desired business vision.

Expanding that metaphor, a business plan is actually like a meta-roadmap in that it refers to, and relies upon, more detailed plans or "maps" for specific aspects of your business, such as finances, marketing and legal. You could think of the business plan like the map of the entire U.S.A. — it gives you an overview of the country, but to navigate around a specific state, you will want to work from a more detailed map. The U.S.A. map is needed to give you the overall plan or strategy; the state maps help you execute your plan.

Your business plan moves you toward your business vision and is the starting point for various other plans, such as your financial plan (also known as a budget or financial forecast), your marketing plan, and your operational plan.

If all this talk of multiple plans is bringing on a panic-attack, take a deep breath and relax. Planning is neither hard nor painful. It really doesn't take much time, and it will actually *save* you time. A rule of thumb in the corporate world is that every hour of planning saves you four hours of execution. This is because the process of thinking through and developing a plan results in your being better prepared to take effective and efficient action; you'll know what steps to take so you can better focus your energies and attention. In other words, taking action without a plan is typically not an efficient use of time, nor is it effective.

It's recommended that a business plan be developed before you start to heavily invest in your new business, in order to determine if it is a good fit with your personal goals, situation, and lifestyle. For the coaching profession, this investment is typically the cost of your initial coaching skills training and minimal start-up expenses.

Another rule of thumb is to develop the business plan six months before you plan to start your business (assuming you are working another part- or full-time job at the same time). However, if you are already in the midst of or have completed your basic skills training, or if you are already a paid coach, it's not too late to create a business plan! Regardless of the timing, your business plan will be worth the effort.

Like your business vision, your business plan will take some time and energy to create, and it will also be a continually evolving document. Changes in your business vision, your target market, your areas of interest, or your financial goals will all translate into changes in your business plan.

Business Plan Overview

If you pick up six different books on business plans, you will find at least six different plan formats. Again, there is no single right format. However, the structure I present here is one that I have used with small service-oriented business owners and entrepreneurs (including coaches) that has proven valuable and easy to use.

For each of the topics listed below, I also show which chapter(s) covers the topic in greater detail. Just by working through this book and workbook, you will be creating your business plan.

1. Business vision (Chapter Two)
2. Your services and/or products
3. Business name (Chapter Twelve)
4. Marketing plan (Section Four), including:
    * Your niche
    * Your brand
    * Your pricing strategy
    * Factors that will influence your business (e.g., economy, seasonality)
5. Legal aspects (Section Two)
6. Financial projections (Section Three)
7. Available resources, including:
    * Your own strengths and weaknesses (Chapter Eleven)
    * How much time, energy, financing you can put into your business (multiple chapters)
    * Your team of advisors
    * Other resources available to you, or that you need
8. Upcoming business goals and milestones (Chapter Eleven)

In the workbook are exercises and worksheets to help you develop your business plan.

Should You Be Self-Employed?

You are embarking on a journey to become not only a coach but also a self-employed entrepreneur. This is a big step! You may love being a coach but realize that you don't want, or are unable, to be self-employed. Clearly, determining if you want to be self-employed is a key decision.

Being self-employed is heaven for some and hell for others. When compared to being an employee, self-employment typically offers greater freedom, creativity, and variety, but also brings greater risk, additional responsibilities, and more work. As with so many things in life, it is a tradeoff.

Here are some characteristics of being a self-employed coach that you may want to consider:

1. Typically for the first year or more, your business may not be profitable. The initial investment in training, marketing, and other start-up expenses may outweigh your coaching income for a period that will vary from case to case. Answering the following questions will bring you additional clarity and will also feed into your financial plan:
   * How much money are you able to invest in starting your business (including training expenses)?
   * How long (number of months or years) are you able to wait until your business is profitable?
   * Once your business is profitable, what is your target net revenue (total coaching revenue minus all business expenses) per month?
   * How realistic are your financial expectations? Talk to several experienced coaches to determine if your financial projections are overly optimistic.
2. Starting a business takes time and energy. If you have other demands on your time such as a part- or full-time job or family responsibilities, you will need to be realistic in determining the number of hours you can spend

on your business. These work hours will be used for any activities associated with the business such as training, planning, marketing, client sessions, and administrative activities. Your answers to the questions below will also be used in your six-month action plan.

- For the next six months, how many hours per week are you able to invest in your business?
- Do you have enough energy and stamina to work this number of hours on your business?

3. Being a self-employed coach is, by and large, a solitary business. In a way, this is ironic since many are attracted to the coaching profession because of their strong people skills. However, many practicing coaches state that feelings of isolation and lack of a support structure are two of their biggest challenges. Although you will be coaching clients, your interactions with them will be focused solely on them and their goals. It's not a reciprocal relationship; they are your customers. In addition, being self-employed means that you will no longer have a boss or manager or co-workers to motivate, support, supervise, and guide you.

- How do you feel about working by yourself most of the time? This is an especially important question if you are extroverted and need interaction with others to help structure your thoughts and move into action.
- Can you motivate and manage yourself? Structure your time and stay focused? If these are not strong skills for you, look for ways to strengthen and augment your skills, such as additional training and/or hiring a business coach to hold you accountable for your goals and progress.

Once you've answered the questions above, if you still feel that self-employment and coaching are the right path for you, then let's get started on building your business plan.

Covering the
Legal Bases

The pessimist sees difficulty in every opportunity.
The optimist sees the opportunity in every difficulty.

SIR WINSTON CHURCHILL

W^{E NOW SHIFT OUR FOCUS} from the internal to the external world, specifically the legal and regulatory aspects of our business world. Just as every human baby involves some paperwork and recommended tasks, like a birth certificate and vaccinations, so too does your new business "baby." These aspects of your business will be on-going, but the peak of activity is typically within the first year or two of starting out.

The topics in this section — business legal structure, licensing, insurance — can be a rude awakening for the new coach. A question I have often heard is "Do I *have to* do these things?" No, you don't *have to* do anything in this section, or in this book. You always have a choice. You have made a choice to start a business, and this book covers what is involved in establishing a legal, successful coaching business. You can choose to skip steps and ignore requirements. That choice may save you a bit of time, a bit of money, and perhaps allow you to avoid tasks about which you have some fear or dislike. It's your choice. The result will typically be increased financial risk for you and your family, such as potential penalty fees, higher taxes, loss of personal assets, loss of income, perhaps even loss of the business. Granted, the probability of these things happening are very small, but they can and do happen.

I don't want to sound foreboding or heavy-handed, because a coaching business is fundamentally a low-risk venture. However, I am baffled by people who automatically handle the legal aspects of their personal life — valid driver's license, auto and home insurance, social security number, marriage license — and yet they choose to disregard similar guidelines and requirements for their business. I just don't get it. Do you not get married because it takes time and money to get a marriage license? After all, you can live together and not be married, just as you can do business without a business license. You just wouldn't be doing business legally.

As you go through the topics in this section, I ask you to remember that you are the CEO of your business. How do you want to be as CEO? From that perspective, what choices are in the best interest of you and your business?

5

Which Business Structure?

*One day Alice came to a fork in the road and saw a
Cheshire cat in a tree. Which road do I take?
she asked. Where do you want to go?
was his response. I don't know, Alice answered.
Then, said the cat, it doesn't matter.*

LEWIS CARROLL

WHEN YOU START YOUR BUSINESS, you need to decide which
way you want to go in terms of a legal structure. The
typical options for a small business includes:

- Sole proprietorship
- Partnership
- Limited Liability Company (LLC)
- S-Corporation

You should have a basic understanding of each structure,
along with its advantages and disadvantages, and then pick
the one that best meets your current needs. With few excep-
tions, there is no wrong choice but the best choice isn't always obvious. As your business grows, you may decide to
"upgrade" from one structure to another.

At the end of this chapter, in Exhibit 5-1, is a table with a high-level comparison of the structures. You may, after reading this section, decide to seek guidance from a lawyer or an accountant.

This chapter will also briefly discuss two additional structures — the C-Corporation and the Limited Liability Partnership — to provide insight into why these structures are not recommended for a coaching practice.

Each of the structure options has advantages and disadvantages, mostly having to do with the effort and expense to establish and maintain the company, and the amount of personal liability that you assume for company operations.

All four options have the advantage of "flowing through" the business' net income (gross income less deductible business expenses) to the owner, or members, of the company. This is a desirable feature as it reduces the overall amount of tax you pay.

In other structures (such as C-Corporations) income is taxed both at the business level and then again when it is paid out to you as salary or dividends. This means that the business income is, in effect, taxed twice!

Sole Proprietorship

This is the most common legal structure for coaching businesses. A sole proprietorship has only one owner (or a husband and wife who file taxes jointly) and may or may not have employees.

Advantages

- Easiest business structure to set up since there are no special forms to establish the company.
- Least expensive business structure. No additional state fees or taxes are charged to be a sole proprietor.
- Taxes are filed using Form 1040 Schedule C or Schedule

C-EZ, both of which are straightforward and relatively simple tax forms that are filed with your personal tax return.

- In most cases, sole proprietors are not required to get an Employer Identification Number (discussed further in Chapter Seven) because the owner's personal Social Security Number can be used to identify the business.

Disadvantages

- There is no distinction, in both tax and legal terms, between you personally and your business. Your are the business and the business is you. A sole proprietor accepts the risks of business to the extent of *all* his or her assets, whether the asset is used in the business or used personally. You would be personally liable for any judgment against your business, meaning that your home, savings, car and other personal effects can be seized. Also, a judgment against you personally could impact any business assets. Although the risk of being sued may be fairly small, it does exist. It is important to remember that you do not need to do anything wrong to be sued.
- Any audit of you personally would also audit your business (and vice versa), since the personal and business tax returns are so closely linked. The percentage of tax returns audited has been found to be higher for a Schedule C than for other business-related tax forms such as the 1065 form used for partnerships and LLCs.

Bottom line: A sole proprietor structure is quick, easy, and inexpensive to set up, but it involves higher personal risk.

Partnership

A partnership is the relationship existing between two or more persons who join together to carry on a trade or business.

Each partner contributes money, property, labor, or skill, and expects to share in the profits and losses of the business. Partners can be individuals, corporations, trusts, estates, and other partnerships.

Advantages

- Allows you to establish a business with another person(s) providing additional resources (for example, capital, experience, and labor).

Disadvantages

- Allowing another person into your business always opens the door for dissension. Finding a compatible business partner takes time, effort, patience, and compromise. Many partnerships fail due to disagreement between the partners.
- Unless specifically set up as a Limited Partnership, a partnership is a General Partnership, in which case all partners are liable for the entire debts and obligations of the partnership. This means that each partner is personally liable for the actions of themselves *and* the other partners. The legal term for this relationship is "joint and several liability," meaning that the liability to any one partner is not proportional to their fault. Any judgments against the business can seize your personal assets if necessary, similar to the sole proprietorship.

  In a Limited Partnership, at least one person needs to be a General Partner. Limited Partners may invest in the business but can not be involved in management or providing service and are liable only to the extent of their investments.
- An Employer Identification Number is required (discussed in Chapter Seven). In addition, business-specific financial accounts (e.g., checking account) are needed (discussed in Chapter Eight).
- Requires federal tax form 1065 — Partnership Informa-

tion Return — to be filed separately from your personal tax forms. In addition, a simple K-1 form needs to be prepared annually for each partner. These forms are similar to W-2s or 1099s in that they document the amount of income (or loss) flowing to the individual from the business (discussed in Chapter Nine.)

- A written contract or Partnership Agreement is not required to form a partnership, but it is highly recommended to record the basic partnership terms such as roles, responsibilities, expectations, and division of income and expenses.
- Compared to the sole proprietor structure, there is slightly more paperwork to setup and maintain.

Partnerships allow you to have business partners, which can be a great asset. But that asset comes with an inherent risk since all General Partners become personally liable for any debts, actions, or judgments against the business and the other partners.

Limited Liability Company (LLC)

An LLC is a hybrid entity combining the characteristics and benefits of both the corporation and the partnership. This structure is a relatively new business entity that has become more popular with small business owners in the past ten years. An LLC has one or more "managing members" (owner-managers) and may have one or more non-managing members (owners but not managers).

Each state has different statutes and laws that govern the establishment of an LLC so it is essential that you determine the specifics for your state. In addition, it's not necessary to establish your LLC in your state of residence. Having an out-of-state LLC is a bit more complex, but it may be a desirable option for financial reasons (i.e. less expensive to establish).

From a tax perspective, LLCs can be treated either as a partnership or as a corporation. When you set up an LLC it is important to designate that you want partnership treatment in order to get the "flow through" benefit. Since the LLC laws and forms are state specific, this designation process varies by state. Two common places to look for this designation are on the LLC forms filed with the Secretary of State and also on your state's LLC tax forms and tax returns. In this book, the term LLC refers only an LLC that is classified as a partnership for tax purposes.

The LLC provides the benefits of a corporation (limited personal liability for the members) with the tax benefits of a partnership (net income is taxed only at the personal level and not at the business level). The term "limited liability" means that each LLC member will not be personally liable for the LLC's debts or other obligations. Members are at risk for the amounts that they have invested in the LLC but are shielded from the LLC's creditors and legal judgements against the company. However, given the small size of your business, you may need to personally sign for any business loans or credit cards.

Advantages

- The LLC structure affords a high degree of personal liability protection, provided that the separation of your personal and business finances and activities remains clear.
- The limited liability aspect of this structure protects your personal assets from any judgment against your business. The company is seen as distinct from you personally, both from a tax and a legal perspective.
- In most states, LLCs can be used for businesses with only one managing member (owner). At time of printing, a few states still require two or more owners.
- If you are a one-person LLC, the IRS treats the LLC as a sole proprietorship from a tax perspective. You can then

use Schedule C or C-EZ along with your personal 1040 form, if you choose to.

- Relative to an S-Corporation (discussed next), the LLC is less restrictive in terms of allowable members and other structural details. For example, distribution of net income (or loss) is flexible with an LLC, but is more restricted with an S-Corporation.

Disadvantages

- Compared to a sole proprietorship or a partnership, the LLC structure has more paperwork to establish the business. You need to file a form (typically a one-page Articles of Organization) with the Secretary of State to establish the LLC, and pay an annual tax to the state.
- The IRS allows LLCs to be taxed either as a partnership or as a corporation. As stated earlier, you will need to determine how to designate partnership tax treatment. This will allow the net income from the business to flow to your personal statement, and not be taxed at the business level.
- Uses federal tax form 1065 — Partnership Information Return — to be filed separately from your personal tax forms. Some states have a unique tax form for LLCs, while others use the same form for both partnerships and LLCs. In addition, a simple K-1 form will need to be prepared annually for each member of the LLC. This form is similar in intent to W-2s or 1099s in that it documents the amount of income (or loss) flowing to the individual from the business.
- An Employer Identification Number is required (discussed in Chapter Seven). In addition, business-specific financial accounts (i.e., checking account) are needed (discussed in Chapter Eight) and extra care is required to keep business and personal finances separate.
- You (with the other members, if any) should create an Operating Agreement outlining roles, responsibilities,

and expectations of LLC members. In addition, you will need to satisfy a few legal requirements, such as having an annual meeting with documented minutes (even if you are a one-person LLC).

- If you want to use a state-licensed profession within your coaching practice — e.g., therapist, CPA, attorney, nurse, or teacher — you cannot use the LLC structure. To retain the feature of limited personal liability and use your state license as part of your coaching business, your only option would be the S-Corporation structure.

- LLCs must have a finite lifespan that, in many states, cannot exceed 30 years.

- Since this is a relatively new structure, the LLC-related statutes and laws are still new and mostly untested. Lawyers and CPAs may be unable to provide clear advice since there is minimal case law to provide guidance or precedence. In addition, many books and resources focus mainly on sole proprietors and corporations with little attention given to LLCs.

- Also because of its relative newness, some business forms or documents (e.g., credit card applications) do not yet provide an "LLC" option when asking for your business structure. When filling out a form that doesn't provide an LLC option, the closest choice is a partnership.

It is not surprising that the LLC is gaining popularity. Although the structure does require some initial effort and time to set up (about eight to twelve hours), it is low maintenance once established.

S-Corporation

The corporation is the most complex of business structures. As defined by Justice Marshall's famous decision in 1819, a corporation is "an artificial being, invisible, intangible, and existing only in contemplation of the law."

The S-Corporation was introduced in 1986, and has also been called a Sub-Chapter S-Corporation. It was developed specifically for small businesses, to create a less cumbersome corporate structure relative to a standard C-Corporation. The S-Corporation has stockholders who are owners, and managers (who may or may not be stockholders) running the business. In the scenario of a one-person coaching business, you would be the sole stockholder (owner) as well as a manager.

The S-Corporation enjoys the benefits of incorporation (limited personal liability) but is taxed as if it were a partnership.

This structure is popular for closely held businesses (i.e., not publicly traded and often a family business), for state-licensed professionals (such as CPAs, lawyers, therapists, nurses), and for those companies planning to eventually transition to the C-Corporation structure.

Advantages

- In many states, an S-Corporation can have just one stockholder (owner). At time of printing, a few states still require two or more owners. (Check with your Secretary of State.)
- Provides the limited liability associated with a corporation or an LLC, and the flow-through tax treatment associated with a partnership or LLC.
- Can be used by state-licensed professionals who are unable to utilize the LLC structure.
- Corporations have an unlimited lifespan.

Disadvantages

- The paperwork required for the establishment and maintenance of an S-Corporation is slightly more complex than for an LLC. To establish an S-Corporation, you file papers with the Secretary of State (several page Certificate of Incorporation). In addition, you file IRS form

2533 — Election by a Small Business Corporation — to elect an S-Corporation status.

- Requires an annual form to continue the pass-through tax treatment. These forms must be filed by a specific date each year for it to be effective for that year. If the forms aren't filed, the company will be taxed like a C-Corporation (meaning that the profit will be taxed twice, once at the business level and then again at the personal income tax level).
- There is an annual tax to the state.
- Compared to an LLC, there is much less flexibility on how income (or loss) is distributed among the shareholders (owners).
- Uses federal tax form 1120S — U.S. Income Tax Returns for an S-Corporation — filed separately from your personal tax forms. This is true even if you are a one-person S-Corporation.
- An Employer Identification Number is required (discussed further in Chapter Seven). In addition, business-specific financial accounts (e.g., checking account) are needed (discussed in Chapter Eight).
- Similar to an LLC, you should document roles, responsibilities, and expectations of the stockholders (owners). In addition, you will need to satisfy a few legal requirements, such as having annual meetings with documented minutes.
- This type of structure has numerous technical rules and constraints, such as having fewer than 75 stockholders.

With the advent of the LLC, the S-Corporation structure is losing its popularity. But it is still the structure of choice for many state-licensed professionals, for family businesses, or for those companies that plan to eventually transition to a standard C-Corporation structure. On a day-to-day basis, the S-Corporation is quite similar to the LLC.

C-Corporation

This structure is designed for large, publicly held companies. It is mentioned here to point out why it is not a recommended structure for a small coaching firm.

- Double taxation: net income is taxed both at the corporate level and then again when you pay taxes on your salary and dividends.
- Extensive and complex government regulations: There are multiple reports, forms, and legal requirements from all levels of government (local, state, and federal).

Limited Liability Partnership (LLP)

Like the LLC, the LLP is also a relative newcomer. Laws and regulations concerning LLPs vary state to state. In most states, the LLP structure can only be used by public accountancies and law firms. In general, an LLP is a General Partnership that has registered with the state as an LLP. Being an LLP provides the partners limited personal liability for debts, obligations or liabilities of the LLP or other partners. However, the partners are still personally liable for their own personal actions, debts, and obligations.

Changing Structures

Your initial choice of a business structure doesn't have to be permanent. You can start out as sole proprietorship and later convert your business to a partnership, an LLC, or an S-Corporation. The easiest conversion is from a sole proprietor structure to any of the others. Before you make your decision, it is recommended that you seek guidance from a knowledgeable lawyer or accountant.

Exhibit 5-1. Business Structure Comparison Table

Feature	Sole Proprietor	Partnership	LLC	S-Corp
Net income is not taxed at the business level	✔	✔	✔	✔
Structure can be used by businesses with only one owner (varies by state)	✔		✔	✔
Business is a legal entity separate from the owner		✔	✔	✔
Owner is personally liable for the business	✔	✔		
Owner has limited personal liability			✔	✔
Need to file forms with the Secretary of State to establish the business			✔	✔
Additional annual state tax or fee (varies by state)			✔	✔
File taxes with personal tax form	✔		✔ (one person LLC)	
Uses separate federal tax forms for the business filing		✔ (1065)	✔ (1065)	✔ (1120S)
State-licensed professionals allowed	✔	✔		✔
EIN required	In some cases	✔	✔	✔
Separate financial accounts needed		✔	✔	✔
Need to document roles of each member		✔	✔	✔
Annual meeting required of members and owners with documented minutes			✔	✔

6

Insurance

The superior man, when resting in safety, does not forget that danger may come. When in a state of security he does not forget the possibility of ruin. When all is orderly, he does not forget that disorder may come. Thus his person is not endangered, and his state and all their clans are preserved.

CONFUCIUS

THERE IS A COMMON MISCONCEPTION that if you are a one or two person business working out of your home, that you don't need any additional insurance. Unfortunately, this is wishful thinking and in most cases is not true. Please don't assume that any of your personal insurance will cover your business; the vast majority do not.

Insurance is a form of risk management, which in turn is a way to protect your business and personal assets. As a coach you face certain risks, some of which you can insure against and some of which you cannot. Changes in business conditions that negatively impact your business cannot be insured against. But events such as fire, theft, liability, accidents, or disability can be insured against. Preventing the risk in the first place is, of course, the best form of protection. However, not all risks can be avoided so planning to absorb any risk that occurs is your next best alternative.

For the purposes of this chapter, it is assumed that you already have personal policies for basic home/apartment, auto, personal property, and personal liability insurance. This chapter will cover the incremental insurance needs that your business presents. In addition, the topic of personal health and disability insurance will be discussed.

What Insurance Do You Need?

If you are thinking that your business is already covered by your personal policies, the chances are very high that you're mistaken. Most personal policies will not cover any liabilities, actions, accidents, equipment, or property used or damaged in the course of your business. It is important to review your current policies and verify their coverage.

It's one thing to consciously decide to take your chances by not being insured, but it's quite another to discover that you needed insurance for a risk you didn't realize you were taking, or worse, to assume that you're covered when in fact you're not.

There are three kinds of business insurance that are most important: general business liability, business property, and auto. Why are these important? For the following reasons:

- You may have in-person interactions with clients such as intake sessions, coaching sessions, or workshops.
- If you provide corporate coaching, you might coach your clients at their work site or in your office.
- You may drive to and from client sites and may have clients or business associates in the car with you.
- You will have various pieces of equipment (for example, telephone, computer, printer, books and resources, fax machines, PDAs) used in the course of your business, both in your office and potentially on the road.

The need for other types of business insurance — Professional Liability (also known as Errors and Omissions or E&O) and Business Interruption — depends on the amount of specific risks you take in your business and your personal situation. I recommend that you first understand the purpose of these types of insurance and then determine if they are needed for your business.

You should also review your personal insurance policies when you become self-employed, specifically your health and disability insurance. You may get sick or injure yourself at any time. A broken arm or burst appendix can cost thousands of dollars in doctor and hospital fees. In addition, 20% of people become disabled between the ages of 35 and 65. If your coaching practice is your sole source of income, disability insurance is very important. As your business grows, it is wise to re-examine your insurance coverage and increase your limits and/or add supplemental policies.

Bottom line, it's wisest to never assume you're covered for business purposes on any personal policy, because the chances are high that you aren't. Review your existing policies and work with a knowledgeable insurance professional to determine what business risks are not covered.

Finding the Right Insurance Agent

You may want an insurance agent to help you review your current policies and point out areas of overlap or uncovered risks. This person may also be able to locate additional or less expensive policies that will address your needs. Since small business insurance is considered a specialty item, find an agent that is familiar with small business insurance needs and potential sources.

There are two primary types of insurance agents: independent and captive. Independent agents are able to sell insurance from a variety of companies, whereas captive agents sell for only one company (such as Allstate or Farmers). Working with an independent agent is recommended, as all the special needs of your company may not be satisfied with one insurance company. An independent agent has greater flexibility to find the best coverage at the best price.

Here are some tips to find an agent to work with:

- Ask family, colleagues, friends, and acquaintances who have small businesses.
- Ask the agent or company that provides your personal insurance for a recommendation.
- Search business and trade association literature to see if they sponsor insurance programs for small business or home-based business, or if they have a relationship with a specific insurance company.

Insurance Terminology

The terms "coverage limits," "deductibles," and "exclusions" are critical aspects of any insurance policy.

Coverage Limits

A policy coverage limit is the maximum dollar amount of coverage you can receive for claims within a policy period. In some cases, this limit may exclude or include certain charges.

Deductibles

The deductible amount is what you pay out of your own pocket for an insured incident. In general, the higher the deductible amount, the less financial risk there is for the insurance company. Therefore higher deductibles typically reduce the policy premium (your monthly or annual expense). Policy deductibles may apply to each claim separately or to your combined annual claims.

Exclusions

These are events, causes, or charges that are not covered by the policy. For example, most property policies will not cover earthquake or flood damage, since they are covered by separate policies. In health insurance, there may be exclusions for previously existing illnesses or specific types of illnesses. In some cases, the exclusions are not obvious, so make sure to ask your agent.

General Business Liability Insurance

General business liability insurance provides for protection if you are held liable for property damage and/or personal injury (either physical injuries or injuries such as libel or slander) in the course of your business. It's nicknamed "Trip and Fall" insurance, and that aptly describes its major use. I believe that it's important business insurance to have if you do any in-person work.

In corporate coaching, your clients may request that you have a general business liability policy with a $1 million coverage limit before they will contract with you. This is a very standard request, and the $1 million legal liability limit is not considered high or unreasonable even for a one-person business. General business liability coverage is not expensive, especially when included in a bundled policy (approximate total cost of $250 a year).

Even if you don't do corporate coaching, general business liability insurance may still be prudent. Here are some scenarios to illustrate this point.

- You may be legally liable for damages even in cases when you used "reasonable care." This means that even if you did nothing wrong, you could still be held liable. An example would be if you lead a workshop at a hotel and a participant slips and breaks a leg. You could be named, along with the hotel, as a defendant in any resulting lawsuit.

- Your local clients come to your house for an intake session, and perhaps for quarterly in-person sessions. If your client injured himself while at your home, it would be considered a business-related liability and would not be covered by your homeowner's policy.

- You can be liable for the acts of others under contract to you or working with you, such as partnering with another coach, consultant, or therapist to provide a workshop, seminar, or to perform team coaching.

Even if the suit against you is false or fraudulent, the liability insurer typically pays court costs, legal fees, and interest on judgments in addition to the liability judgments themselves.

With our culture becoming increasingly litigious, general business liability insurance is a relatively inexpensive way to protect yourself (and your personal assets) from a variety of potential issues. However, be aware that it will not cover you in cases where you are found liable for providing a product (such as advice, direction, or guidance) that is found to be defective, negligent, or incorrect. This type of situation is covered by Professional Liability Insurance, which is discussed later in this chapter.

Business Property Insurance

Basic homeowner's policies are not designed to cover the business use of a home. The typical homeowner's policy may only provide $2,000 coverage for business property on premises, and no coverage for liability. A personal umbrella policy won't help as it only covers you personally and not your business. So what are your options?

- Review your existing policy carefully. Your homeowner's/apartment dweller's policy may have enough business property coverage to replace your business assets. If your only business assets are a phone, some files, and some books, then a limit of $1,000 for business property would be adequate.
- Talk with your agent (or view your insurance company's web site) to see if a Home Business endorsement (also known as a "floater" or "rider") is available for your policy. Typically, this endorsement would add a small amount of business property coverage onto your existing policy (e.g., from $2,000 to $5,000). Business property endorsements may cost as little as $15 a year.
- Look into one of the bundled insurance packages discussed later in this chapter. These packages include larger amounts for business-related property (e.g., $10,000) in addition to business liability coverage (up to $1 million) and business interruption insurance. These policies can cost as low as $250 a year.
- If you travel for work, you may want to get an additional policy for any equipment (e.g., laptop, overhead projector, PDA, mobile phone) that travels with you. This type of policy is typically called Inland Marine or Mobile Property.

Automobile Insurance

If you have any vehicles that are used *primarily* for business purposes then you will need a business auto policy for the vehicle. This situation is most applicable if you have an auto dedicated to the business, such as a delivery van. This type of auto insurance requires that the vehicle be registered in the company's name.

More likely, you probably use your personal car for business purposes, such as driving to a client site or a networking meeting. In this case, you need to make sure that your auto policy will protect you in case of an accident while working. This typically requires changing the classification of your car's use from "pleasure" or "commute" to "business use/personal." This doesn't require any special registration, but may increase your annual premium by a few dollars. Be aware that any personal or business property stored in the automobile and not attached to it (e.g., laptop, cell phone) is typically not covered under an auto policy. This situation would need an Inland Marine or Mobile Property policy.

Business Interruption Insurance

This type of insurance will cover any lost income and/or fixed expenses that would continue if a disaster-related event shut down your business. This type of insurance is especially important if your coaching business is the sole source of income for your family. Typical features include:

- Payment of the profits you *would have* earned, based on your financial records, had the disaster not occurred.
- Coverage of business operating expenses that continue (for example, telephone service and loan payments) even though business activities have come to a temporary halt.

An "Extra Expense" policy is also available and covers:

- Reimbursement for a reasonable amount spent, over and above normal operating expenses, to avoid having to shut down during the restoration period. This insurance is useful if you have another location that you can temporarily use while your business is re-opening.
- Only those expenses that help to decrease business interruption costs.

In some instances, extra expense insurance alone may provide sufficient coverage, without the purchase of business interruption insurance. A qualified insurance agent can help you with that decision.

Make sure that the policy limits are sufficient to cover your company for more than a few days. It can take several weeks (or months) to reopen a business after a fire, flood, or other catastrophic event. The policy premium is typically related to the policy limits and the risk of a fire or other disaster damaging your business premises.

Bundled Insurance Plans

The different types of insurance discussed so far (except auto) can be bundled together. Buying a package policy rather than separate policies may provide broader coverage at a lower price. Below are descriptions of two common packages.

In-Home Business Policy

Due to the growing number of home-based businesses, the insurance industry has created this package policy. Typically, for about $250 a year you can insure your business property for $10,000. General liability insurance, up to $1 million limit, is also available. Business interruption insurance, limited coverage for loss of valuable papers and records, accounts receivable data, and equipment is also typically included. Specific coverage and premiums for this type of policy vary greatly across insurance companies so make sure to get several different quotes.

Business Owner's Package Policy (BOP)

This policy has been created specifically for small businesses that operate in more than one location or manufacture products outside the workplace. The coverage is very similar to the In-Home policy, but it increases the liability limits and adds coverage for inventory, as well as broadening the coverage in the other areas.

Health Insurance

If you are leaving your full-time job to start a coaching practice, or you are working a part-time job that does not offer benefits, you will need to secure your own health insurance.

It's important to know that as a business owner, you are no longer covered under Worker's Compensation, which is designed to cover only employees. Therefore if you are injured while conducting business, your personal insurance will have to cover the costs.

The good news is that, starting in 2003, you're able to deduct 100% of the amount paid for medical, dental, and qualified long-term care insurance for you, your spouse, and your dependents.

Sources for Health Insurance

There are three basic alternatives for getting health insurance:

1. If your spouse has health insurance, the least expensive (and easiest) route might be to get added onto that policy.
2. Find a group policy through a professional or business organization (e.g., your local Chamber of Commerce, or National Association for the Self-Employed). Typically group rates are less expensive than buying an individual plan.
3. Purchase an individual plan from an insurance company or insurance agent.

You'll have to determine which alternative best suits your needs. Individual plans (option #3) need to go through medical underwriting, which means that the status of your health may impact whether you are accepted into the plan. In contrast, a group plan (option #2) usually can't turn you away because you have health problems (this varies by plan, so make sure to ask). In addition, group plans typically must meet stricter state and federal guidelines about the coverage they offer.

Look at your cash flow when determining your deductible. If you are able to afford the risk, increasing your deductible from $100 to $2,000 may cut your premiums in half. In some cases, you can save money by opting for a health plan that does not cover your routine doctor visits and medical tests — a policy known as catastrophic coverage.

Be sure to use your state's Department of Insurance as a resource as well. Some states publish health plan shopper's guides, and every state should be able to tell you whether an agent or insurance company has had any complaints filed against them.

Health Insurance Structure and Terminology

There are four principal types of health insurance coverage: basic plans, major medical plans, PPOs, and HMOs. In addition, there is a supplemental option called a Medical Savings Account.

Basic plans, often called catastrophic coverage plans, generally cover only hospital expenses or surgical expenses, or both. They usually don't have a deductible and may reimburse up to 100% of the covered expenses, up to a relatively low maximum amount ($10,000 to $100,000).

Major medical plans typically provide broader coverage than the basic plans, but often do not cover preventative care. They have a deductible each calendar year and will reimburse 50-80% of the covered expense, depending on the service provided and the specific policy, up to a relatively high maximum amount ($500,000 to $1,000,000).

Both major medical and basic plans contain a number of excluded expenditures and procedures. In addition, major medical plans will not cover some expenses if they are over "reasonable and customary" charges for your geographic area.

Major medical plans also vary in their handling of *preexisting conditions,* which are often defined as a medical condition (injury or illness) that required treatment (or was known about) during some period of time (e.g., three or six months) prior to the effective date of the coverage.

Most major medical plans have a limit on the insured's out-of-pocket expenses per year, also known as a coinsurance cap or stop-loss limit. This limit ranges from $1,000 to $3,000 depending on the plan. Once that limit has been reached, all eligible expenses above this amount are paid in full by the plan, up to the overall limit of coverage.

You may be eligible to open a *Medical Savings Account (MSA)* if you are self-employed and have a health plan with a high deductible. An MSA is a tax-exempt account with a financial institution in which you can save money for future medical expenses. The benefits of an MSA include tax-free interest on your contributions, the ability to claim a tax deduction for your contributions, and that the contributions remain in your account from year to year until you use them. You need to meet several rules before you can start an MSA, so check with your bank (or other financial institution) to see if you qualify.

A *PPO (Preferred Provider Organization)* is a variation of the major medical plan. In a PPO, if you use one of the preferred doctors or facilities, the plan will pay a higher percentage of the expenditure, e.g., 70% for a non-PPO doctor but 85% for a PPO doctor.

With *HMOs (Health Maintenance Organizations),* there are several differences. Often there is a small co-payment for each doctor's visit or prescription (e.g., $5 to $20). In addition, there may be less freedom of choice of physician since the patient typically has to be referred to a specialist by a primary care physician. HMO coverage typically contains few exclusions and emphasizes comprehensive care, including preventative care.

Disability Insurance

Statistics show that one in five people becomes disabled between the ages of 35 and 65. More Americans have life insurance than disability insurance (about 70% vs. 40%). But being out of work for any length of time can have serious financial consequences, especially if you are the sole breadwinner. If you are unable to work for an extended period of time due to illness or injury, disability insurance will pay you monthly benefits until you are well enough to return to work.

Individual policies vary on when your benefits would begin, how much you would receive, the coverage limits, and how long you would receive benefits. These variations have a major impact on the insurance premiums.

It's best to not use your disability insurance if you are ill for only a short period, such as two months or less. Using your benefits for such a short period could potentially cause your premiums to increase dramatically. Therefore, it is always advisable to have a "cushion" of savings that could cover two months of basic living expenses.

To help determine if you should get disability insurance, you must decide how much financial risk you are willing to assume and can afford. How long can you rely on your savings? How long would it take you to rebuild your retirement account or pay back any debt you might incur while ill? Can your spouse's income cover your lost income?

Annual costs can range from $1,000 to $3,000, depending on the policy and your personal variables. To reduce the premiums, reduce the length of coverage (e.g., from 15 years to 5 years) or extend the amount of time it takes for your benefits to kick in. The standard is 90 days, but you can increase that to six months or even a year. But make sure to have the appropriate savings needed to support that change. You can also exclude certain injuries or illnesses that could increase your premiums, such as a bad back.

Professional Liability Insurance

Professional liability insurance, also know as Errors and Omissions or E&O, is designed to provide coverage for actual or alleged errors, omissions, negligence, breach of duty, misleading statements, and similar claims resulting from the performance or non-performance of professional services. Most policies cover both the defense expenses (e.g., attorney fees, court costs) and settlements or judgments. Intentional wrongdoing is typically *not* covered.

Whether your practice needs this type of insurance is highly dependent on the type of coaching you do, the type of clients and issues you work with, and the level of risk you personally find acceptable. In rare instances, corporate clients may request that you have an E&O policy on file along with your general business liability policy before they will contract with you.

The cost of these policies can run from several hundred to several thousand dollars annually. Home-based coaching businesses have an additional challenge since many insurance companies will not provide E&O for home-based businesses. If you feel that your practice needs E&O coverage, or you have a client that requires it, contact a reputable business insurance professional.

7

More Government Hoops

*It has been said that democracy is the worst
form of government except all the others
that have been tried.*

SIR WINSTON CHURCHILL

AFTER YOU HAVE DECIDED on a name for your business
(discussed in Chapter Twelve), and determined the
legal structure (discussed in Chapter Five), there remain a
few additional tasks to establish your business in the
government's eyes. In this chapter we will cover the Fictitious Business Name, Employer Identification Number, licensing, permits, and zoning.

Fictitious Business Name

A fictitious business name (FBN) is defined as a business name
that does not include the surname (last name) of all owners
of a business. The purpose of the FBN petition process is to
let the public know who is behind the business name. Depending on the state, these adopted business names will be
called "assumed names" or "fictitious names."

If your business name includes your surname (and you are the sole owner), for example Kelley Coaching, you probably don't need to complete the FBN process. However, if your business name does not include your surname, like Clarity In Action, then you will need to file a Petition of Fictitious Business Name with the County Clerk's office. The specific regulations, form name, and government filing entity will vary so investigate what is appropriate for your location.

The FBN petition process requires that a simple form be filled out (usually with your County Clerk) and that local newspaper notices be run for a specific period of time (typically once a week for four consecutive weeks). There is a cost to the process, both to file the form with the County Clerk and also to run the newspaper notices (about $100 total). However, newspapers vary on their charge to run the notices, so be sure to compare costs. The County Clerk should provide you with a listing of acceptable newspapers. Those newspapers will be familiar with the requirements for the FBN notices, such as the format of the notice, number of times to run, and location in the newspaper.

In most states, you will be unable to open a bank account in the business' name without the approved FBN paperwork. You can also be fined if you are found to be doing business without having the FBN on file at the County Clerk office.

You should file for an FBN within 40 days of starting your practice, and the petition is typically valid for five years. The start date for your business is the day you received your first business revenue.

Employer Identification Number

The IRS assigns Employer Identification Numbers (EINs), which are free, nine-digit numbers with the format 00-0000000. EINs can also be referred to as Tax Payer ID numbers (TINs).

The name is a bit of a misnomer as you don't need to be an employer to need an EIN. In general, the IRS uses the EIN to identify taxpayers required to file various business tax returns. EINs are used by employers, some sole proprietors, LLCs, corporations, partnerships, nonprofit associations, trusts, estates, government agencies, certain individuals, and other business entities.

You can think of the EIN as a unique numeric identifier that refers specifically to your business, much like your Social Security Number uniquely refers to you.

Does your business need an EIN?

- Partnerships, LLCs, and S-Corporations all must have an EIN.
- You need an EIN if you have a Keogh retirement savings plan (discussed in Chapter Ten) or have employees.
- If your business is a one person LLC or a sole proprietorship, and you have no employees and no Keogh plan, you may use your personal Social Security number in place of the EIN.

When do you use an EIN?

- When you open a business account at a bank, credit union, or mutual fund
- On the business tax returns, tax payments, or other tax forms (e.g., 1099s)
- On invoices and contracts with clients

Filing for an EIN

You can easily get an EIN by phone, fax, or mail. All requests require IRS form SS-4, which you can download from the IRS web site (www.irs.gov), or by calling (800) TAX-FORM. Also look at IRS publication 1635 (also available through the IRS web site) which has all the info you might need about EINs and their use.

Once you complete the form, the fastest way to get your

EIN is to call 866-816-2065. You'll get your EIN over the phone. Mailed-in requests may take four weeks to process. Visit the IRS web site to get more information. Use the search function to find the EIN section.

Licensing and Permits

Licensing and permit requirements exist at all levels of government: federal, state, regional, county, city. Unfortunately, they each have different requirements, so you will need to check directly with your specific government agencies to determine what is required.

State

- Many professions and selected businesses are regulated and licensed by the bureaus or divisions of the State Consumer Affairs Department. At present, coaching does not require any state licensing.
- If you plan to sell any taxable products (for example, books, video tapes, or audio tapes), you will need a sales tax license, plus a seller's permit or resale license. These can be obtained either through your state's Board of Equalization or Treasury department.
- If you want more information, call the Small Business Division of your state's Department of Commerce to get a handbook on any state license or permit requirements. Another resources is your local Small Business Development Center.

County/City

- Call your City and/or County Clerk to determine specific requirements for your location.
- At a minimum, business licenses are required for most businesses located in a city or doing business in a city.

Contact the licensing department of the city in which your business is located or being operated. If your business will be based in one city, but you plan to operate in several cities (e.g., on-site corporate coaching), you may need a license from each city. To be sure, check with the tax and license division in each city where you intend to operate.

- Business licenses are typically not required in unincorporated areas (any area outside a city limit), but counties may have restrictions and require permits on some types of businesses. Therefore, you may need both a business license from the city and a permit from the county. Contact your county's Planning Department and County Clerk to find out the specific requirements.

Zoning Requirements

"Zoning" refers to the approved type of business or residence in a given geographic area such as light industrial, manufacturing, rural or heavy residential. Typically, zoning restrictions won't prohibit using a home for a business, but might instead list specific approved businesses or the vague "customary home occupations" which is open to a wide range of interpretations. The restrictions may limit the amount of car and truck traffic, outside signs, on-street parking, number of employees, or percent of floor space devoted to the business.

The level of enforcement varies greatly, and neighbor complaints trigger most investigations. It is best to first check that your residence is zoned for home-based business. To do this, contact the Planning Department of the city if your home is located inside the city limits, or the County Planning Department if your home is in an unincorporated area. If you find that the wording is vague, talk with other home-based businesses in the area, and talk with your neighbors.

The risk of complaint/investigation is typically related to how visible or intrusive your business is to the rest of the neighborhood. If you use common sense and are a good neighbor, you will minimize your risk of zoning complaints.

In addition to city and county zoning, there are private land use restrictions through homeowner, condo, or co-op associations. These restrictions might be found in the following type of documents: property deeds (restrictive covenants); subdivision covenants, conditions, and restrictions (CC&Rs); planned unit development rules (PUD); condo regulations; co-op regulations; and leases. These restrictions and rules are often more strict than the county or city ordinances, and are often more diligently enforced.

Financial Matters

To fulfill a dream, . . .
to be given the chance to create,
is the meat and potatoes of life.
The money is the gravy. As everyone else,
I love to dunk my crust in it.
But alone, it is not a diet designed
to keep body and soul together.

BETTE DAVIS

ONE OF THE BASIC RULES OF ACCOUNTING is Profit = Revenue minus Expenses. So you only have two ways to increase your profit: increase revenue and/or decrease expenses. (See how easy accounting is?) Increasing revenue involves two additional components: the number of clients you have and/or how much you charge them.

In Section Four, which deals with Marketing, we'll discuss ways to increase your number of clients. In this section, we'll focus on the expense side of the equation — how to manage and minimize expenses (including taxes) — along with short trips into the topics of invoicing, taking credit cards, and saving for retirement.

8

Money Management

We make a living by what we get,
we make a life by what we give.

SIR WINSTON CHURCHILL

MANAGING YOUR COMPANY'S FINANCES is as vital to its success as managing the marketing or legal aspects. Without money management, you won't know if you are making a profit or where you are spending your hard-earned income.

The good news is that having up-to-date figures and reports is easier and faster than ever before. With the introduction of several easy-to-use personal computer financial management programs along with credit cards that may automatically download transaction information into your financial management program, the hours spent manually tracking your income and expenses is a thing of the past.

You may choose to hire a bookkeeper or accountant to manage your finances. That's fine! At a minimum, however, you should be familiar with typical financial records and transactions so that you are able to understand your financial reports as well as judge the effectiveness of your bookkeeper's or accountant's services.

In this chapter we'll cover record keeping, budgeting, financial accounts, invoicing, and accounts receivable.

Record Keeping

Practically speaking, you need to keep good financial records to prepare tax returns, determine your profitability, and apply for credit cards or loans. The typical types of financial information to manage include:

- Cash flow — will you have enough cash to cover your bills this month?
- Expenses, either with cash, check, or charge. Which expenses occur each month? Which expenses occur only once?
- Time and expenses to be billed to clients.
- Invoices to clients and payments received.
- Profitability — are you making any money?
- Banking transactions — deposits, withdrawals, and any fees.

Financial Management Software

Although it is possible to keep your financial records with pencil and paper, the availability and low cost of computer-based financial systems make manual record keeping inefficient. Using a computer-based system will make the sometimes-tedious task of record keeping much easier, faster, and less stressful. There are several personal computer programs that can track your business finances efficiently and effectively. Some of the most popular include: Intuit's Quicken for Home and Business; Intuit's Quickbooks; Peachtree Accounting.

The same program can often be used to track both personal and business finances, although it is strongly recommended that the data be kept in two separate files. If your company is a partnership, LLC, or S-Corporation, you *must* keep the data files separate to clearly differentiate between your personal finances and your company's.

All the programs listed above include the ability to write

checks, create and track invoices, track and categorize expenses, and have multiple report formats such as Profit & Loss Statements and Balance Sheets.

If your company is a sole proprietorship, some programs are able to transfer your business-related financial information directly into personal computer-based tax programs. For other business structures, this information transfer is done manually based on information readily found in the company's Profit & Loss and Balance Sheet reports.

Billable Time and Expenses

An important component of record keeping is for billable time and expenses. There are several ways to accomplish this task, based on the number of clients you have at any one time.

- If your client sessions are mainly standard weekly sessions, one option is to track the hours and expenses per client on a sheet of paper. You can create a time tracking format in a word processing or spreadsheet program. Save the monthly form for your records (both for tax purposes and also for your coaching credentials). An example form can be found in the workbook.

- A more sophisticated option is to maintain these records in a time tracking program on your personal computer. These programs, such as TimeSlips, allow you to set up your clients, specific billing rates, your hours and expenses per client and the program will total and track the amounts. This method of time and expense tracking is very helpful if you have a really large number of clients that you meet with irregularly, especially corporate clients, and have related billable expenses.

Leaving a Paper Trail

Even in this computer age, the IRS still requires a hard copy backup for most financial transactions. Your challenge is to implement a process to retain and organize your receipts.

There are no set rules, just the need to establish and maintain a timely, well documented, and organized paper trail. Find the process that works best for you.

Here is one option for handling this task. Purchase a twelve-section partitioned accordion file to store your business receipts. Each partition could represent one month of the year or one type of expense, such as auto, meals, or travel. In addition, set up a centrally located, easily visible basket or container. Each day put all of your business receipts into that basket or container. This minimizes the chance of losing any receipts. When you sit down to enter your financial information (once a month, at a minimum), remove the receipt from the basket, enter the information, and then file the receipt into the accordion folder. At the end of the year you will have one file that contains all of your business receipts for that year.

Budgeting

Before you set off on a trip, it's useful to have a map. A budget is a critical piece of the map to the destination of having a successful and profitable business. In more practical terms, a budget is a projection of income and expenses for a specific period of time. Your budget will tell you approximately how much money you will need/want to spend, which in turn will tell you the amount of income you need to earn.

The best way to make sound business decisions is to make a budget and then follow it. However, a budget is just a plan, and life doesn't always go according to plan. Perhaps you'll get three more clients or there might be an unexpected expense. Whatever the change, keep your budget up-to-date with this new information. For this reason, always make budgets either in pencil or in your computer, where the information can be easily modified. It is helpful to save copies of your budget during the year so you can later review how it changed and the reasons why.

As you create your budget, you'll find that you won't have all the figures you need. When this happens, use your intuition or just make a guess. Don't let not knowing stop you! In the companion workbook, some example figures have been provided as estimates, but remember that the numbers may vary based on your location, the needs of your practice, and your local and state regulations.

To help you create your budget, a blank budget form can be found both in the workbook and online at www.thebusinessofcoaching.com on the "Additional Resources" page.

Within your budget, you will have sections for three major categories: Income, Start-up expenses, and Ongoing expenses.

Income

This is the money you are paid for your coaching services or related activities such as book sales, presentations, or workshops. Your monthly forecast will vary based on the number of hours you work and your other activities.

If you have clients now, you can use your current income as a base amount, and then increase the monthly amount depending on when you plan to enroll additional clients. If you don't have any clients, you will need to estimate your income figures. These income estimates will be a key input into your marketing plan (Chapter Eleven). Here are some considerations:

- In general, it may take two to three months of marketing and networking to find your first client.
- Determine how many hours a week you can work on your business. This estimate needs to include time for your clients as well as for training, marketing, and administrative activities. By reviewing the number of hours needed by your practice, you can then determine if the forecasted

number of billable coaching hours is realistic.

- A full coaching practice is typically 20 clients, though there are some experienced coaches who can handle a larger number. Twenty clients require approximately 12 to 15 hours a week for the coaching sessions and for any client-specific paperwork. However, only ten of these hours would be billable.
- In addition, plan at least four to ten hours a week for marketing and administrative activities. If you do in-person coaching, make sure to include your travel time.
- Lastly, include any hours for continued training or work towards certification.
- The International Coach Federation (ICF) conducted a survey and found that trained coaches charge, on average, about $200 a month for two hours of coaching. These charges range from $100 to $600 or more a month, depending on niche, skill level, and type of coaching offered (personal, corporate, or executive).
- Reread "Knowing Your Value" in Chapter Three to further help you define your fee structure.

Business Start-Up Expenses

Business start-up expenses are those expenses that you incur *before* you actually begin coaching for pay. Why track them separately? Because the IRS treats start-up expenses differently than other business expenses. You are not able to deduct the full amount of your start-up expenses in your first year of business. Instead, they must be amortized over 60 months, meaning that you deduct the expenses in equal amounts over a period of 60 months. (Amortization is discussed further in Chapter Nine.) Because of this IRS rule, it may be advantageous to get your first paying client before you begin spending much money on the business.

If your business has start-up expenses, you may want to develop a separate budget just for that time frame. You could use the same expense items listed below, but they would occur only during the start-up period. Once the start-up period has ended (i.e., when you get your first paying client), you can then use your ongoing budget.

Ongoing Business Expenses

How much money will you need to spend? One of the biggest mistakes a new business owner can make is failing to anticipate expenses. Certain expenses will be necessary to establish and run your coaching business. Use your budget to help you plan ahead. In the first year or so, you may not make a profit each month, and it is better to anticipate those lean times, rather than be surprised when they arrive.

Below are typical business expense categories and some examples.

- Advertising (e.g., Yellow Pages, ads in newsletters)
- Auto expense (e.g. gasoline, repairs, insurance), based on the percent of business miles over total miles driven
- Bank charges (e.g., fees for your business account)
- Books and resources
- Business insurance
- Business meals (only a portion is tax deductible)
- Conferences and conventions
- Credit card annual fees (business credit cards only)
- Duplication, fax, printing expenses
- Gifts (limited to $25 a year per recipient)
- Health insurance (medical, dental, and qualified long-term care for you, your spouse, and dependents)
- Internet access and email services
- Interest and debt payments on business loans
- Legal and licensing fees (e.g., LLC fees, Fictitious Business Name, resale license)
- Marketing expenses (e.g., brochures, fliers, business cards, logo design, web site design and development)
- Miscellaneous expenses (at least 10% of total expenses)
- Office assistance

- Office equipment (e.g., furniture, computer hardware)
- Office rent
- Office supplies (e.g., folders, paper, pens, batteries)
- Parking and tolls
- Postage and shipping
- Professional development (e.g., training, seminars, and workshops to improve your coaching skills)
- Professional dues (e.g., International Coach Federation)
- Professional services (e.g., accountant, business coach, lawyer)
- Rental fees for equipment or for post office box
- Taxes (estimate at 25% of net profits)
- Telephone charges for your business phone (or business calls from your home line)
- Travel expenses (e.g., air, hotel, taxi, train)
- Web hosting service

Use your budget as a management tool, comparing budget vs. actual expenses at regular intervals (quarterly at a minimum.) A budget is useful only to the extent to which it helps you plan ahead. If your budget is no longer an accurate predictor of your income and expenses (i.e., a deviation more than 15% over or under), then you need to revisit and revise your numbers.

Financial Accounts

If your company is a partnership, LLC, or S-Corporation, it is seen as a legally separate entity from yourself. Because of this you *must* establish separate financial accounts for your business.

If you are a sole proprietor, the need to establish separate financial accounts is more a matter of preference. It is recommended (but not required) to keep your personal and business accounts distinct and separate. This separation makes record keeping much simpler and allows you to separate business-related and personal expenses easily so that you can monitor your cash flow and profitability. In addition, the separate accounts will facilitate tax return preparation.

Bank Accounts

One of the initial steps in establishing your business is to open a business bank account. The personal funds you put into this account will be the "seed money" to start your business and will represent your beginning equity.

After you have received your Fictitious Business Name approval and your Employer Identification Number (both discussed in Chapter Seven), you can establish an account in your company's name. The account should use your company's EIN number for identification instead of your personal Social Security Number. (If you don't have a company name, just use your personal name and Social Security Number.)

The first type of account you will need is one that allows check writing so you can purchase goods and services for your business. Many larger financial institutions now have web and phone access for bill payment, which saves you the time and effort of writing and mailing the check. As your cash reserves grow, you may want to open up a second account, such as a money market account, so that your money can earn interest. In addition, you may want an account to regularly save for your tax payments.

Credit Cards

Business credit cards can be obtained from multiple sources. Again, these should be set up under the company's name. Typically the issuing organization will require that you personally sign for any credit card liabilities. If you use Quicken to manage your business finances, there is a Quicken business credit card that will download the credit card transactions into your Quicken files. This feature greatly decreases administrative overhead. (Quicken contact information is located in the workbook.)

Use credit cards wisely! The typical interest rates are very high, and if you pay only the minimum amount each month, the goods and services you buy will double in cost in typically less than eight months.

Line of Credit

If you know that major expenses are coming up, and you don't have adequate cash flow, a good option to pursue is a business line of credit from your financial institution or commercial bank.

A line of credit is different than a loan. With a loan, you are given a check for a stated amount of money and you pay interest based on the full loan amount. In contrast, a line of credit allows you to use as much or as little of your credit limit as needed. Since you use only as much money as you need, when you need it, your interest payments are minimized.

Another advantage of a line of credit is a lower interest rate relative to credit card interest. However, you do need to plan ahead as a line of credit may take up to four weeks to approve and fund. But once you get the line of credit, it might take only a phone call to make the funds available. As with business credit cards, you might be required to personally sign for the liability.

Invoicing

Invoicing your clients and receiving payment is like oxygen — your business can not survive without these activities. For you to be a successful coach, you must have income. For you to have income, you must invoice your clients and they must pay you!

Why take the time to send invoices? Here are some important reasons:

- An invoice is the legal document that shows that payment is due to you. If you don't send invoices, and you have a non-paying client, you have no recourse since you haven't sent any legally-recognized notice of their outstanding payment to you.
- An invoice is a reminder to the client that payment is due, including how much and by what date.
- Companies that send invoices are perceived to be more professional and business-like.

Invoicing is a straight-forward process that, once established, takes little time. Here is a suggested structure for your invoicing process:

1. During the coaching session in which you discuss the following month's schedule (typically the third week of the month), let the client know that you will be sending them an invoice for the following month.
2. Prepare and send your invoices at the same time each month, such as during the third week of the month.
3. Make sure your invoice includes a payment due date. Typically this would be a date about two weeks from the date you mail the invoice. You may need to send invoices earlier in the month to accommodate a longer travel time (e.g., from California to New York or Europe). You can reduce the amount of travel time by sending email invoices.
4. Clearly state that if you do not receive the bill by the due date that any subsequent sessions will be canceled until the payment is received. Be firm about this! In addition, include the same wording in your coaching agreement and mention this policy during your intake session. If the client has an excuse why they can't send the payment, reassure them that the coaching sessions can start again just as soon as you get the payment. You

are not firing the client and you are not being a heartless person! Instead, you are being a smart business owner by stating that you do not work for free, and you are being a good coach by holding the client accountable for their actions (or lack thereof).

5. When you get the payment, leave your client a quick voicemail or email thanking them for their payment and reminding them of the next session. If you don't get the payment, then leave your client a voicemail or email letting them know that you haven't received payment yet and that you will be happy to re-schedule the session once payment is received.

6. Don't work for free more than one session. You are a business owner, and as such you are responsible for ensuring the profitable success of your practice.

The actual format of the invoice is not critical, though it should include several pieces of information:

- Your company name, address, and phone number
- A numbering system for tracking invoices
- The billing date and the payment due date
- The name and address of the person to whom the invoice is sent
- A description of the services being invoiced, e.g., "Personal coaching services for August, 2003" plus the number of hours included and your hourly rate
- The total amount due on the invoice
- Your Employer Identification Number or your Social Security number (only if you are a sole proprietor)

The invoice should look professional and be easy to understand. Your financial management program may have a standard invoice format and may allow you to customize the format and add your company logo. Alternatively, you could use a word processing or spreadsheet program to create a standard invoice template. Invoices don't need to be hardcopy, so you can create an email invoice template that you reuse each month. Whatever method you choose, make sure to keep a copy for your records. An example invoice is included in the workbook.

Accounts Receivable

Once you've mailed an invoice, it becomes an "account receivable," which is an accounting term meaning money that is owed to your business for services or products. The goal is to "turn" your accounts receivable as quickly as possible, meaning that payments from clients should be received in a prompt fashion.

Checks

Currently most payments are made by check. There are three main drawbacks to payment by check: the large number of days from sending the invoice to receipt of payment, the additional overhead to deposit the checks, and the potential for bounced and lost checks.

Credit Cards

The ability to accept credit card payment offers your clients a great convenience and also benefits you by reducing the time lag between billing and receipt of funds. But there are costs associated with accepting credit cards, and there are a variety of companies offering services. Let's first go over the terminology and fee structures associated with accepting credit card payments, and then discuss some alternatives suitable for a coaching business.

TERMINOLOGY AND FEES

A *Merchant Bank* is a financial institution that focuses on products and services for businesses. Many large banks have both a merchant division and a consumer division. Your personal bank account is a consumer product. Your business checking account is probably a merchant product.

A *Merchant Account* allows you to accept credit card payments and submit credit card transactions. You deposit the credit card payments into your merchant account like you deposit checks into your business checking account.

A *Credit Card Processor* is a financial institution that does the processing of credit card transactions. These processors are typically a merchant bank or are associated with one.

Credit card transactions can be either *swiped* or *non-swiped*. A swiped transaction requires physical possession of the credit card, for example in a retail store where the cashier physically swipes your credit card through a machine (called an *electronic authorization terminal*). Non-swiped transactions are those where the card is not present, such as transactions conducted by phone, fax, email, mail, or Internet. In these instances, the merchant does not physically possess the credit card, so the information is manually keyed into a secure Internet web site connected to the credit card processor. Merchant banks typically focus on swiped transactions due to their higher volume. However, for most coaching practices, non-swiped transactions are the norm.

An *Online Payment Service* is an alternative to having a merchant account, and acts as a middleman between you, your client, and the credit card processor. When using an online payment service, you do not collect or input credit card information. The transactions are handled between the payment service, your client, and the credit card processor. You would not need a merchant account, nor a credit card processor. Your tasks would be to initiate the payment cycle (i.e., send an invoice) and subsequently pay the online payment service for their services.

Discount fees are what you, as a business owner, pay the credit card processing company or online payment service to process a credit card transaction. There are typically two parts to the fee: a percent of the payment amount (*Discount Rate*) plus a per-transaction charge (*Per Item Fee*). There is a wide range of discount fee structures between service providers. In addition, there may be a *Minimum Monthly Discount Fee*, which is the minimum amount of monthly discount fees. Even if you have no transactions in a month, you will still pay that minimum amount. There are several instances where the discount fees are typically higher:

1. Online payment services typically charge a higher fee than a standard merchant account
2. International credit cards, i.e., issued by a bank outside of the U.S.
3. American Express transactions have a slightly higher discount fee than MasterCard or Visa

Along with the discount fees, there are additional types of charges. A *Statement Fee* is the charge for a monthly summary statement, showing the details of your transactions. A *Gateway Fee* is the monthly charge to access the secure Internet web site used to input and transmit credit card transactions. These two charges can each range between $5 and $25 a month. Many service providers also charge a *Set-up Fee* to establish your account, ranging from $100 to $500.

Based on my experience with my own merchant account, I pay a total of about 7% of my total credit card revenue to cover all of the various charges and fees, and that does not include the initial set-up fee. Accepting credit cards is definitely a convenience, but it does have a significant cost.

CREDIT CARD PROCESSING OPTIONS

Once you have decided that you want to accept credit cards, your next decision is: Do you want your own merchant account, or do you want to use an online payment service?

With your own merchant account, you would have your client fill out a Credit Card Authorization Form, typically during the intake session. With this information, you are able to bill the client's credit card directly by entering the credit card information and dollar amount through an Internet-based secure server (a gateway) which is connected to the credit card processor. From the client's perspective, it appears that they are billed automatically each month with no effort on their part. This option requires that you establish a merchant account with a credit card processor.

Practice Pay Solutions is one business that is familiar with the credit card processing needs of coaches and can set up your merchant account (www.practicepaysolutions.com). PPS focuses on professional associations and their members in industries that typically have non-swiped transactions, such as coaches and speakers. PPS is not a merchant bank, a credit card processor, nor an Internet gateway. Their role is to find the best merchant account services, bring them together into a package and act as a one-stop shop for purchasing and setting up your credit card processing.

With an online payment service, you are hiring a company to act as your merchant account and handle all the transactions between the credit card processor and your client. Typically, with an online payment service, you would email an invoice to your client and provide a link to your online payment service web site. Your client would log onto that web site and enter the payment information. The payment service would notify you when the funds were transferred to your account, and would bill you for their services. As you can see, using an online payment service requires additional steps on the part of the client, which may delay the payment process. Also, if you sell products or services in person (such as coaching sessions, workbooks, audio tapes, or books) or via your own web store, an online payment service isn't very efficient, as all transactions require the customer to log directly onto the online payment web site.

Here are brief descriptions of two potential online payment services.

- PayPal, www.paypal.com, is a low cost option for accepting credit card payments. With this service, you send an invoice by email to your client with a link to the PayPal website where your client would pay the invoice. Two slight disadvantages to this option are that you are not able to accept American Express Corporate Cards, and that your client would need to "join" PayPal (i.e., fill out a one-page personal information form online) and store their credit card information online in PayPal's secure server.

- Acteva, www.acteva.com, offers online payment services targeted primarily for events and activities. The typical listing on Acteva is for discrete (i.e., non-recurring) events, such as workshops, sports events, presentations, seminars, and annual dues for professional organizations. However, you can set up a listing where the activity is "Monthly Coaching Sessions." Much like PayPal, your client would sign on to the Acteva web site to pay for that activity. Acteva does not require the payer (your client) to "join," nor is their credit card information stored online. However, this service is more expensive than PayPal. However, when you set up the activity listing, you are able to designate whether the transaction fees are to be paid by the client or to be deducted from your payment. In this way you could have the client pay for the added convenience.

Enabling your business to accept credit cards can be a potentially intimidating process involving new terminology, varying fee structures, and multiple players (e.g. credit card processor, Internet gateway, merchant bank) — similar to the situation discussed for Internet Service Providers (Chapter Sixteen). When comparing the different credit card processing options, make sure to answer the following questions:

1. What types of transactions do I need the credit card

processing for — monthly invoices, in-person sales, web store sales, registration for workshops, others?

2. What specific service(s) does this service provider offer?

3. What are *all* the fees for this service (e.g., monthly, per transaction, flat fee and percentage, startup, annual)?

4. What other service providers will be needed to complete the transaction, and what are their fees? Do you need to contact the other service providers directly, or will this service provider handle that interaction?

5. Will this service provider support the account long-term, or is their role primarily a sales function for other companies? If they will handle the account long-term, how comfortable do you feel with their customer service abilities?

Barter

Another form of payment is barter, which is the exchange of products or services without the use of money. Typically you "sell" your coaching services and in return can "buy" other services or products. Income generated through barter must be reported and is taxable. A few bartering tips:

- Be clear about the retail value of your services.
- Barter only where the value of your services is matched by the value of what you are receiving. In other words, if you barter two months worth of coaching (with a value of $400), and receive only $200 of products or services in trade, you will be working for half-price.
- Research the typical cost of the products or services you are receiving for the barter. In this way you avoid "paying" more than you should.

9

Business Taxes

*It's getting so that children
have to be educated to realize that
"damn" and "taxes" are two separate words.*

SOURCE UNKNOWN

E VEN THOUGH YOU DON'T WANT TO, from your first day of
business, you need to be thinking about taxes, specifically how to minimize them and how to track all of your
expenses and income. Being organized during the year will
make your annual filing go more smoothly and quickly!

The subject of taxes is broad and complex. This chapter
will provide information on just the basics of business taxes,
giving an overview of what you are entitled to under the law.

Business Deductions

In general, your deductions will fall into one of three categories: ordinary business expenses, depreciation/amortization,
and home office expenses.

Ordinary Business Expenses

These expenses are necessary for the operation of your business. You will need to have documentation to support all

your business deductions, so save your receipts. Below is a listing of common business deductions.

- Accounting/bookkeeping fees
- Advertising expenses
- Automobile expenses (only the percent that is used for business)
- Bank charges and fees (only for business accounts)
- Books and periodicals
- Business/trade conventions
- Business gifts (annual limit of $25 per recipient)
- Business meals (50% is deductible)
- Computer, printer, software, and related equipment (if used over 50% for the business)
- Depreciation and amortization
- Dues for professional and trade associations
- Education expenses for maintaining or improving required skills
- Insurance premiums (business, medical, dental, and qualified long-term care for you and your family)
- License fees and taxes
- Merchant account or credit card processing fees
- Office furniture and equipment
- Office supplies
- Online services used for the business (including email)
- Parking and tolls
- Postage and shipping
- Printing and duplication
- Self-employment taxes
- Start-up expenses (amortized over 60 months)
- State and local taxes on the business
- Preparation of business tax return
- Professional services (e.g., lawyer, coach, accountant)
- Telephone expense (only your separate business line or individual business calls if using your personal line)
- Travel expenses

AUTOMOBILE EXPENSES

Whenever you leave home for business-related activities, you are on a business trip. Even if you happen to stop by the grocery store in the course of the business activities, it is still classified as a business trip. If the automobile you use for business is also used for any personal travel, you will need to keep a log of your business and non-business travel.

At the end of the year, you can either determine the percent of miles that were business-related and deduct that percent of your auto expenses, or you can deduct the standard IRS deduction per business mile ($0.36/mile for year 2003). Parking and tolls are not included as automobile related expenses and should be deducted separately.

OFFICE EQUIPMENT

For your computer and related equipment, the business use must be 50% or greater to qualify as a business deduction.

Depreciation and Amortization

To depreciate means to spread the deduction over the life of the purchased item rather than deducting the entire cost in one year. For certain types of expenses you have the choice of either depreciating the cost over several years or expensing the cost all in one year using a Section 179 capital expense deduction. Your decision on which option to use may be influenced by your current and anticipated future income levels. For example, if you purchased new office furniture and know that your income will be higher next year, you may choose to depreciate the office furniture over three years to get the tax benefit of the deduction spread across three years. Alternatively, if your income is quite high this year, you may want to write off the entire cost this year, using a Section 179 capital expense. However, this deduction cannot exceed your net income for the year, and any amount over your net income is carried forward into the following year's taxes. Each year there is a limit on the amount of Section 179 deduction allowed, which is $25,000 for year 2003. Types of items that can be depreciated include office and computer equipment and furniture. Depreciation rules are fairly convoluted, so you would need to consult appropriate reference material or a tax accountant for additional assistance. As mentioned in Chapter Eight, amortization is a similar concept except that there is no physical object to depreciate. Start-up costs are an amortized expense, meaning that you deduct the total costs over a 60-month period.

Depreciation and amortization are called "paper expenses" in that there is no cash transaction involved. Your annual depreciation and amortization expenses are calculated at year's end.

Home Office Expenses

The primary tax advantage that sole proprietors have as a home-based business is the home office deduction. This deduction allows you to deduct the cost of operating and maintaining the part of your home that you use for business. But this deduction comes with some fairly stringent criteria. If you think that you are eligible and want to claim this deduction, I recommend that you consult with a qualified tax accountant. This deduction is available only for sole proprietors and one-person LLCs that file using the 1040 Schedule C. There are two main criteria that must be met in order to qualify for this deduction:

1. The part of your home you wish to claim as a business expense must be used *exclusively* and *regularly* for business.
2. The part of your home you use exclusively and regularly for business must be one of the following:
   * your principal place of business, or
   * a place where you meet with customers or clients in the normal course of business, or

- in connection with your business, if you use a separate structure that is not attached to your home, or
- for the administrative or management activities of your business and you have no other fixed location where you conduct substantial administrative or management activities of your business.

"Exclusive use" means that the portion of your home you're claiming as a deduction is used *only* for business.

"Regular use" refers to using the business space on a continuing basis, not just occasionally.

"Principal place of business" means that the location must be the place where the most important functions of the business are performed.

"Meet with customers and clients" unfortunately refers to in-person meetings, not telephone calls.

"For the administrative and management activities" is a recent addition to the criteria and offers an opportunity for the corporate coach to qualify for the deduction.

If you qualify for the home office deduction, you may be able to deduct a variety of expenses such as portions of your mortgage interest (but not the principal), home related taxes, and utilities. There are numerous rules associated with the deduction, and if the eligibility is not clear, the presumption is that the home office does not qualify as a deduction. The expenses would be filed on tax form 8829.

There are two major disadvantages to this deduction:

1. Due to the high potential for abuse, the IRS reviews these deductions *very* carefully. Although it can't be confirmed, it is widely felt that taking this deduction is a "red flag" which may increase the chances of an audit.
2. Claiming these expenses will have implications if you plan to sell your home while your business is still operating. Consult a knowledgeable tax accountant for additional information.

Estimated Tax Payments

When you were an employee, your estimated federal, state, Social Security and Medicare taxes were taken out of each paycheck. Now that you are self-employed, you will need to make quarterly estimated payments to cover these taxes. These payments are made by you, personally, and not by the business, since all the business income flows through the business to you. You will need to make payments both to the IRS and to your state tax department.

To avoid any underpayment penalties, you need to make four estimated tax payments each year: April 15, June 15, September 15 and January 15. Notice that these dates are *not* equally spaced apart and plan accordingly. There are specific estimated tax payment forms that come with instructions in federal form 1040-ES.

There are several options as to how much to pay each due date.

- One possibility is to not pay anything! Just expect a big tax bill along with underpayment penalties when you do your annual return. The penalties aren't really steep, as they are based on current prevailing interest rates. You could look at the penalties as the "interest" the IRS or state tax department is charging you for the "loan" of your tax payment amount. (Penalties are not tax deductible.) You might choose this option because your coaching income is minimal, or for cash flow reasons.
- To avoid the underpayment penalties, you should pay the previous year's business tax amount in equal installments at the due dates. This works well when your income is increasing each year as you only pay last year's tax amount even though you are making more money this year. Come April 15, when you send in your annual filing, you will have to send in the incremental tax amount owed.

- Another method requires you to estimate how much you will make during the current tax year and calculate the tax on that income and pay a large percentage of the tax as quarterly payments.

If you use TurboTax or other tax software to handle your annual filing, it may have the functionality to calculate estimated tax payments. Two other options would be to hire a tax accountant to complete the forms for you or to work with a tax accountant to have your calculations checked. In addition, the IRS web site has very useful information including some well-structured tax guides (www.irs.gov).

1099 Forms

As a business owner, you may be sending out and/or receiving 1099-MISC forms. These forms are similar in concept to the W-2 form you received as an employee: they record the amount of money either paid out to or received from an individual or company.

Issuing 1099s

You should file form 1099-MISC whenever your business pays a person or small business over $600 for services (which may include parts and materials). Here are some examples:

- You hired a local graphic artist, who is an LLC, to design your logo and business card for $800.
- You hired a consultant to set up your office computer network for $650. The consultant is a partner in a partnership.
- You have a business coach, who is a sole proprietor, to help you maintain clear focus on the management issues of your company. You have paid the coach $2,400 this year.

- You hired a college student as an independent contractor (not an employee) to assist you in basic office work. Over the course of the year you have paid her $1,600.
- You hired an attorney to file your LLC papers and assist in the setup of your company. The attorney was part of a law corporation. The fees were $700.

The common elements to these examples include:

1. The services were performed for your company, not for you personally. Although you made the contact with the service provider, negotiated fees, approved the work, and ultimately made the payment, you performed these actions as the owner of a business. (The example of the coach is a legitimate business expense if the focus of the coaching included the success of your business, and not solely on your personal life.)
2. The service provider was a sole proprietor, a partnership, or an LLC. If the service provider was an S-Corp. or a C-Corp., you do not need to file a 1099 form. (The exception to this rule is attorneys and lawyers, who always get a 1099, regardless of their legal structure.) The terms "freelance" and "independent contractor" should be treated as sole proprietors.
3. The amounts paid were over $600 for the year.

You can get the 1099-MISC form and instructions from the IRS. The form is very simple to fill out, and has duplicate pages that are sent to the IRS, the state (if required), the service provider (two copies), and your files. Typically, these forms need to be sent out by the end of January of the year following the year of the service (e.g., by January 31, 2005 for services performed in 2004). In addition, you will need to file Form 1096 with the IRS, which acts as a summary of the 1099s that you send out.

Due to some special formatting and color printing on the

forms, the 1099 and 1096 forms need to be ordered directly from the IRS at (800) TAX-FORM. Note: Several tax software programs allow you to print off 1099 and 1096 forms from their programs. Although these forms can be used for reference purposes (i.e., you can see the dollar amounts calculated for each box on the form), you are *not* able to send these black and white copies to the IRS.

Receiving 1099s

If you are a sole proprietor, partnership, or LLC and you have clients that have hired you for the purposes of their business, then they should send you a 1099-MISC form if they pay you over $600 in one year. You will use the 1099 form as a double check against your income records and will file it with your records. In some states you may need to file a copy with your state tax return as well.

Annual Filing

Different business structures file different federal tax forms.

- Sole proprietor: 1040 Schedule C or C-EZ
- Partnership: 1065 (plus K-1s to the partners)
- LLC: 1065 (plus K-1s to the members), or 1040 Schedule C or C-EZ for a one-person LLC
- S-Corporation: 1120-S

Your state may require a copy of your completed federal form, or may have a separate tax form. In addition, there may be a state fee (over and above your personal state taxes) for an S-Corporation or an LLC. Typically these fees are paid using a separate form directly to your Secretary of State.

There are several personal computer tax software programs available for doing your business taxes, both at the federal and the state levels. A few of the most popular programs include: Intuit's TurboTax Home and Business (sole proprietors), Intuit's TurboTax for Business (LLCs, S-Corps, Partnerships), and H&R Block's TaxCut.

If you are a sole proprietor, some of the financial management programs mentioned in Chapter Eight can automatically send the appropriate information into the tax software.

If your company is an LLC, S-Corporation, or partnership, the information needed to complete your business tax forms will come from the Profit & Loss report and the Balance Sheet report created by your business financial management program.

The workbook has additional information on personal computer tax software programs.

Self-Employment Tax

If you have been an employee prior to starting your own business, you are aware of the Social Security and Medicare taxes that were withheld from your paycheck. As an employee, you only paid half of the total tax (about 7.5% of your gross pay); your employer paid the other half.

Now that you are self-employed, you have to pay both your personal share and what used to be your employer's share (about 15.3% total). However, a portion of this tax is deductible so the net cost to you is about 12.5% of your net income (gross income less business expenses).

Once your net income reaches $87,000 (the limit for year 2003), no additional Social Security tax is required. However, there is no limit for the Medicare portion and it remains at 2.9% of your net income. These taxes are included as part of your quarterly tax payments and are also calculated on your personal federal 1040 form.

10

Retirement Plans

Retirement at sixty-five is ridiculous.
When I was sixty-five I still had pimples.

GEORGE BURNS

YOU MAY BE THINKING "How can I worry about retirement? I just started coaching!" Well, the time will fly by faster than you imagine and retirement planning is part of being self-employed.

Don't put off saving for retirement or think that it is an unaffordable luxury. With intelligent planning, you can save for retirement while also keeping your new business afloat. It's important to start investing in a tax-free retirement account right away. Perhaps the amount you initially save may not be very large, but the annual amount can increase as your business grows. In addition, the deposits into the account are business deductions, so you don't pay tax on your contributions into the account and all the interest generated is tax-deferred until after age 59½.

So what is the benefit of saving money in a retirement account? More money! Because the interest compounds without taxes, the account will grow much larger much more quickly than if you put the same amount of money into a regular savings account. Let's look at a very simplified example.

Jeff is 30 years old and is able to save $1,000 a year for retirement. He makes about $40,000 a year so is in a 28% federal tax bracket. (For simplicity, we will ignore state taxes.) Jeff can either put his annual $1,000 into a retirement account that makes 10% or into a regular account (i.e., non-retirement) that makes 10%.

Here's the difference in the account balances after 30 years:

- In the regular account, he will have accumulated about $105,000.
- In the retirement account, he will have accumulated about $181,000.

What a difference! But once Jeff retires (age 60), he will start to pay taxes on the portion of the $181,000 he withdraws from his retirement account. Worst case, if he took all the money out in one lump sum and paid federal taxes on the interest, he would have about $130,000 remaining. That is still a $25,000 advantage over the regular account, and represents about a 25% increase over what he would have made in the regular account.

Clearly, with no taxes and compound interest, your money can grow much more quickly! A retirement account makes good financial sense. The more money you are making now (and the higher tax bracket you are in), the more advantageous the comparison between a retirement account and a regular account. If you are already saving money each year for retirement, make sure to put it into an account where your savings can grow the fastest. If you haven't started saving yet — start today!

Each of the plans described in this chapter is available to small business owners. Do some research and/or consult with a financial adviser to determine the best plan for your needs. But start saving as soon as you can. Good web sites to review for further information about different types of retirement plans include fidelity.com, vanguard.com, askmerrill.com (Merrill Lynch), and quicken.com.

SEP-IRAs

A Simplified Employee Pension Plan, commonly known as a SEP-IRA, is a retirement plan specifically designed for self-employed people and small-business owners. Because this type of plan is very simple to set up and to maintain, and requires no IRS reporting, it is one of the most popular plans.

All of the contributions come from the business and are considered business deductions. The amount you can contribute is based on a percentage of the net business income up to 25% or a maximum of $40,000 (for plan year 2003).

The deadline to open and contribute to a SEP-IRA account is April 15 for the previous year, and the contribution amount can vary year to year.

Keogh Plans

A Defined Contribution Plan (Keogh) has two components — the Money Purchase Plan and the Profit Sharing Plan. In some ways, Keoghs are similar to SEP-IRAs but in other ways they are very different.

Like SEP-IRAs, the Keogh plan was designed for the self-employed and small business owner. All the contributions are from the business and are considered business deductions. The amount you can contribute is based on a percentage of the net business income up to 25% or a maximum of $40,000 (for plan year 2003).

However, once the Keogh plan value exceed $100,000, then Form 5500 must be sent to the IRS every year. In addition, you have to determine what percent will go into the Money

Purchase Plan and how much into the Profit Sharing Plan. In general, there is more overhead associated with a Keogh Plan, with little (or no) financial advantage over the SEP-IRA. It is easy to see why the SEP-IRAs are becoming more popular!

SIMPLE IRAs

"SIMPLE" stands for Savings Incentive Match Plan for Employees, and it is a retirement plan for small business owners and sole proprietors who are looking for an effective retirement program for themselves and their employees. This plan allows employers to make contributions into their employees' retirement accounts (matched or unmatched). This is a retirement plan to investigate further if you are an employer, but for a one-person business it is not an optimal choice.

Employee Funded Plans

There are additional retirement plans designed primarily for companies with employees who wish to make pre-tax contributions to their retirement plan. These plans are the Simple 401(k), and the 401(k) plan.

Marketing and Communication

Be daring, be different, be impractical,
be anything that will assert
integrity of purpose and imaginative vision
against the play-it-safers,
the creatures of the commonplace,
the slaves of the ordinary.

SIR CECIL BEATON

U NFORTUNATELY, MANY PEOPLE think that marketing is a dirty word, that it routinely involves manipulation, gimmicks, and unprofessional behavior. While it's true that there are people who employ these tactics, let's not jump to the conclusion that they represent what marketing is really about.

Marketing is an honorable and vital practice. If we removed all marketing from our economy, every business (including government and non-profits) would stop. Marketing is the "language" in which businesses talk with their customers and potential customers.

Simply put, marketing it is the process of making people aware of you and how you can make a difference in their life. That's it. Now you can choose to do this by being manipulative, pushy, and unprofessional if you want, but my

recommendation is that you instead design a marketing program that is aligned with who you are, your values, and your
natural style of interacting with others. Yes, it's true — you
can do that and be successful! In fact, if you try to market
your business in ways that are not reflective of who you are,
you will be frustrated, unhappy, and not successful. So if you
have stories in your head about how you *should* do marketing, or what it *should* look like, please throw them out and
be open to some new ideas.

11

Your Marketing
Plan

*Without goals, and plans to reach them, you are like
a ship that has set sail with no destination.*

FITZHUGH DODSON

MARKETING CAN BE A TERRITORY FILLED with gremlins and assumptions, because we often equate marketing with having to "sell" ourselves, push ourselves on others, or act like stereotypical used-car salesmen. Rest assured that no-one wants you to be a coaching "salesperson"! That would not be effective, and would probably not be a comfortable style for you or your potential clients.

Coaching is an industry that prides itself on authenticity and integrity, and these principles suggest that your marketing reflect who you are and not who you think you should be. Throw out your assumptions about what you think marketing *should* look like! Your most successful marketing strategy will reflect who you are, how you approach the world, and what you stand for.

First, you will need to create a marketing plan. These come in all shapes and sizes, and the framework I present here has been very successful in my own business and with my entrepreneur and small business clients. This framework will help clarify your thoughts, focus your attention and energy, and maintain momentum toward your business goals.

An additional dimension to this framework, one not typically found in the popular marketing literature, is conscious attention to both the doing and the being of marketing. We are very familiar with the "doing" of marketing — networking, speaking, creating marketing materials, giving sample sessions — the various activities we think of when we hear the term marketing. The "being" of marketing has to do with how you are being with yourself and with your potential client while you are engaged in your marketing activities. It is a more subtle and a more powerful aspect of your marketing. How you are being can overpower what you are doing, so it's an important dimension to discuss.

The framework we will discuss contains four steps:

1. Self-Assessment
2. Niche (Target Market) Definition
4. Short-Term Business Goals
5. Short-Term Action Plan

As you work through this framework, make sure to write down your thoughts, ideas, and decisions. In the companion workbook, there are several worksheets that walk you through this process of creating a marketing plan that authentically reflects who you are and your unique style.

Self-Assessment

The success of a coaching relationship is greatly influenced by the experiences and attributes of the coach. When you market your services, the potential client learns about the value of coaching but also, and more importantly, learns about *you* —

who you are, your perspective and attitude, how you act, and whether your personality is a good fit with their's. Because you are such an integral part of your coaching services, it's critical that you conduct a thorough self-assessment to recognize and leverage from your own uniqueness.

Your Unique Attributes

A question I often hear from new coaches is "What makes me different from all the other coaches?" and the short answer is: *you!* You are unique, and your individual mixture of experiences, attributes, skills, vision, passion, and expertise differentiates you from every other coach. So, part of this self-assessment is to look at you — past, present, and future.

Although you might feel that you have no remarkable or unusual qualities, they are there! Often they are related to your life experiences and background that you might take for granted. Here are some examples of unique attributes that might be overlooked:

- A special affinity and rapport with teens
- A previous career in the performing arts enabling you to understand that environment and lifestyle
- Having parented several children, a perspective that allows you to relate to new mothers and the struggles they face
- Several years of small business ownership which has given you knowledge of small business management
- Having worked in the high-tech industry, thereby being familiar with its culture and challenges
- Having experienced the difficulties of divorce, an ability to empathize with others in similar situations
- Strong spiritual beliefs that provide you divine guidance and direction
- Experience, through your personal and/or work life, working with those coping with a family member facing a life-threatening illness

Unique attributes can come from any facet of your life. Your challenge is to recognize them, write them down, and choose the ones you want to leverage in your marketing and your coaching. This is no time to be modest, so let your light shine! Once you recognize and internalize the talents, attributes, perspectives, values, and attitudes that you bring to the coaching relationship, you will have a better sense of who you are as a coach as well as a much easier time enrolling clients. Remember, you are unique!

Spend a few hours on this part of the self-assessment. Not only will it be valuable information for you to be aware of, it will also feed into several other aspects of your marketing plan and activities (specifically your brand). The workbook will help you through the process.

Your Marketing Being

How do you feel, and what do you think about, when you are interacting with a potential client or referral source? Do you have a red flashing sign in your thoughts proclaiming "Now in Marketing Mode"? Do you have a voice in your head saying "Danger! Danger! Marketing! Marketing!" Perhaps you feel embarrassed when you talk about your business and your work as a coach. Do you hold back your passion and enthusiasm, thinking that you have to appear suave, polished, and professional? What might be the impact of these mental and emotional states on how you are perceived? You might be seen as disingenuous, not natural, or "sales-like." In general, not authentic, not enrolling, and not fun for you.

One of the wonderful aspects of being a coach is that the most effective and enrolling way of being is just to be yourself and be a coach. Surprise! All of those coaching skills you've learned and honed will also help you in your marketing.

Here's an experiment: Next time you talk with a potential client or referral source, don't think of it as marketing. Instead, relax, take a deep breath, and just be yourself and be a coach. I can guarantee that your interaction will be much more alive and interesting, and will be more successful than if you try to be a smooth, slick, professional marketing machine. Instead of being in your head, thinking up a clever marketing phrase, or trying to "figure out" your next step, be engaged and focused on your conversation mate. Be curious, ask powerful questions, use your intuition, find out what makes that person come alive. Remember that you have the skills and gifts of a coach. Be generous and share your gift; you don't need to "sell" it. Your powerful coaching plus your relaxed confidence and positive attitude will sell itself. Share your excitement and passion for coaching — it's infectious.

Shifting your perspective about marketing and coming from a more coach-like (instead of sales-like) frame of mind won't result in everyone you talk to becoming a client. But it will make your interactions more authentic, relaxed, and enjoyable for all involved and that means you will be more naturally enrolling. Express yourself authentically and claim them if you want them as a client. At the same time, work to be unattached to their response. Some will say yes and some will say no; that's guaranteed. Being unattached does not mean being apathetic or indifferent, but rather that you don't assign emotional meaning to their answer. If they say yes, great! you have a new client; if they say no, great! you're able to move on to the next person.

Consciously set an intention for how you want to be when you're interacting with prospective clients and referral sources. What impression do you want to leave behind, both mentally and emotionally? How do you want to be perceived by others?

In Chapter Twelve you'll learn about creating your own brand. Include this information in how you want to be with potential clients. Set an intention, write it down, and remind yourself often. Make sure to use the power of how you are "being" to your advantage!

Defining Your Niche

Most successful businesses, in any industry, focus on a specific place in the market. This place might be centered around a narrow set of products (e.g., mobile phones), or a region (e.g., regional grocery store chains), or a set of customer characteristics (e.g., children, the elderly, Hispanics, or new parents). This is called niche or target marketing.

Although our businesses are small, we can apply the same strategy to our own marketing efforts. Defining a niche helps us focus on a segment of the market in which we believe that we'll have success. Contrary to what you might think, choosing a niche doesn't rule out people. Instead it focuses your limited time, energy, and money on proactively reaching out only to those people who are most likely to hire your services. This is not to suggest that you can't have clients outside of your niche! Having a niche means that when you spend your own time and energy actively seeking potential clients, your efforts are focused on a fairly narrow band of the population. It's not humanly (or financially) feasible to market to everyone in all situations.

Some niches are found by serendipity. For example, I never dreamed that I would write this book or be seen as an expert in the business of coaching. It all started with coaches asking me business-related questions, and my desire to answer them in a comprehensive and easy-to-understand manner. After awhile, I realized that I had stumbled upon an unfilled need in the industry and a niche was born.

Other niches are well planned. Many coaches pursue advanced training for specific niches, such as coaching teens or relationship coaching. They define their desired niche and proactively plan their entry into that part of the market.

The process of defining a niche asks: What group should I target and reach out to? Following are some places to look for your answers. In addition, there are several exercises in the workbook to help you further define your niche.

- Look at your everyday life for niches — they surround you all the time. The challenge is to recognize them. What people do you come in contact with on a regular basis? Through your work, church, professional organizations, neighborhood, social groups, volunteer activities? For example, if you've worked as a technical writer for years, then one of your niches might be other technical writers. Look at the contacts you have close at hand (and may take for granted).
- Don't overlook the niche of family, friends, and acquaintances. This niche is typically called your "sphere of influence." It represents the segment of the population that you've met over the years. It isn't a very scientifically designed niche, but it's a powerful one. These are people who already know you and can give you a recommendation or referral. These folks have an interest in your success; after all, you are a relative, a friend, or a colleague. They want to see you succeed! You may decide that you don't want to coach your family and friends — that's fine! Once they understand the power of coaching (based on one or two sessions with you), they can act as referral sources for you, your extended "sales team."
- Think in terms of short-term and long-term niches. Perhaps the idea of coaching technical writers isn't very compelling for you, since you've worked in that industry for so long. But the short-term niche of technical writers could segue into a larger niche of non-fiction writers, which you are excited about. You already have connections with the technical writers, so use them to help gain access to the niche that you find more compelling. This doesn't mean that you can provide the technical writers with poor quality coaching. Far from it! By providing excellent service to the technical writers, your name will travel farther and faster into a wider circle of writers, all of whom are potential clients.

- Look at your business experience and background. A growing niche is corporate coaching, which is focused on a segment of the population (people at work) and which requires a slightly different set of skills, experiences, and services than personal coaching. Typically, corporate coaching focuses on individuals, work teams, managers, or executives and often occurs at the client's site. The corporate coach may spend an entire day on site working with multiple clients within the same company. In general, corporate coaching requires some experience in business, management, and the corporate environment.
- Determine what niche you *want* to work with but don't currently have access to. Don't worry about the access challenge right now. Write down the description of your desired niche and we'll address how to get into that niche later in this chapter.
- In your first year of coaching, you may choose to have a broad niche, such as "folks I meet networking" or "people I meet in my community." This niche strategy is appropriate when you are focused more on developing your coaching skills with a wide range of clients. However, after your first year or so, you will benefit from narrowing your focus and more tightly defining your niche.

Allow yourself to have more than one niche at a time, and recognize that your niches will evolve over time. However, niches do need to stand still long enough for you to focus on them and execute some targeted marketing activities. That length of time might be as short as six months or as long as five years.

Understand that your niches may be in different stages of development at any point in time. Perhaps you've been coaching technical writers for a year now and it's a well established niche for you. At the same time, your efforts in the niche of non-fiction writers might have just begun, involving exploratory marketing activities such as informational interviews, making initial contacts, and checking out various writer associations and conventions.

When you recognize the number and variety of potential niches, you may find that the most difficult aspect of this exercise is selecting just one or two to be your primary focus areas. The exercises in the workbook will guide you through this brainstorming and selection process.

Short-Term Business Goals

As a coach, you know the importance of goal setting for your clients. Now you need to turn that coaching skill to focus on your own business success. As always, the goals should be measurable, action oriented, well defined, realistic, and have a specific timeline.

The planning horizon most appropriate for a small service business is a six-month window. This window is long enough that some long-term thinking is required, but short enough that an action plan can be easily developed.

The nature of your business goals will change over time, based on the stage and stability of your coaching practice. However, remember that your goals will all spring from your business vision and business plan.

If your coaching practice is relatively new, your goals may be related to getting your practice up and running, such as:

- Business is legally established
- Business cards and brochure are complete
- Participating in two networking organizations
- Initial niches defined
- Practice has five clients

If your business is more established, your goals might be related to sustaining and growing your practice. You may be planning to introduce new products or enroll additional clients. Potential goals might be:

- Develop and present "Life in Balance" workshop twice
- Presented four or more times to local organizations
- Practice has 15 clients
- Completed coaching certification program

For right now, don't focus on the specific activities needed to reach your goals. Focus instead on the end-state, the goal itself. Imagine that you can jump ahead six months, what would be different? How would you describe or measure that difference? Choose three to five core goals for the next six months, and have them be as specific as possible. If your goals are too general, you will have a difficult time developing an action plan, and assessing your progress. The workbook has exercises to help develop goals and action plans.

Short-Term Action Plan

Now it's time to translate your goals into an action plan. The recommended format uses two-month time buckets, for example buckets for months one and two, three and four, five and six. There are several benefits to splitting the six-month window into two-month buckets:

- Reduces the chance of procrastination, since there are deliverables due every two months
- Requires that the actions are discrete enough to fit into a two-month bucket, thereby being a manageable size
- Lowers the level of anxiety since your attention will be focused only on a two-month window
- Still allows "wiggle room" within the two-month bucket so you won't feel overly constrained

So what kind of activities might go into this plan? In the

next section you will find a list of various marketing activities that would be suitable for a short-term action plan. When developing your list of activities, be realistic and remember that we all have time constraints. You may want to accomplish 12 tasks within the first two months, but you may not have the time, the funding, nor the energy!

Once you have your short-term goals and six-month action plan, post them in a visible location in your office. The documents will remind you of the goals you are working towards and the key activities for the current month. Share your lists with others — a colleague, a business coach, a friend, a family member. These two steps will have a significant positive impact on your success in achieving those goals.

Once you have completed months one and two, post your list for months three and four, and develop your action plan for months seven and eight. In this way you will always have a rolling six-month action plan. If you don't complete all of the month-one and -two activities, don't beat yourself up. Instead, determine what happened and what needs to change. Adjust your activity plan based on what you learn, and move on. You will be amazed by how much you can accomplish in only four to six months!

If you determine that a new idea or task needs to be added to your plan, take a minute to see how the new idea fits in before you make any adjustments. Ask yourself the following questions:

- How does this new task support your business vision?
- Does the new idea complement the activities you have planned for this month?
- How much time will it take? Will you need to remove an activity to fit in the new one?
- Where does the new idea fit in terms of priority — is it less or more important than those already in your plan?

Marketing Activities

Marketing activities fall into two major categories: direct and indirect. A successful marketing plan needs a mixture of both types, and a rule of thumb is at least three direct activities for every two indirect.

Direct marketing activities are those in which you are directly interacting with potential clients, such as going to networking events and meeting people, or making follow-up phone calls. Direct marketing activities are sometimes more stressful because you are communicating directly with potential clients, but they also provide the biggest payback. Talking with potential clients about the benefits of coaching and your services is where you'll find the most opportunities.

Indirect marketing activities are those that build your name recognition and credentials over a period of time. These activities typically take a longer time to pay off than direct marketing. Examples include speaking engagements, presentations, professional affiliations, writing articles, and publishing a newsletter.

The list below contains over 50 marketing activities (both direct and indirect) with reported success by other coaches. This list is not exhaustive! There are many other ways to market your coaching and this list shows the wide variety of possible activities — there is something to fit every style, budget, and temperament. Don't feel that you need to do every activity listed here. Instead, pick out 10–15 activities that interest you. Try to choose a variety of activities from each of the sections.

Develop Your Network

❏ Attend business networking events such as Chamber of Commerce, Women's Business Network, and Rotary. Plan to meet three new people at each networking event you attend. Always take your business cards.

❏ Attend the meetings of industry or trade organization that might attract potential clients or referral sources.

❏ Be prepared to network at any social, cultural, or sporting event that you attend.

❏ Join the International Coach Federation (ICF) and attend the local meetings and the annual conference.

❏ Introduce yourself to local therapists, psychologists, psychiatrists, and other potential referral sources. Explain the benefits of coaching, your background and niche, and ask them to refer suitable clients to you.

❏ Find a reason to call your past clients — an article to send them or just to find out how they are — and mention that you have openings in your practice.

❏ Every time you meet a potential client, follow up with a personal note. Few people take the time to write personal notes, so your efforts will be noticed!

❏ Mail out an introductory letter and brochure to all the people in your address book. Tell them about coaching and its benefits. Offer a sample session. Ask for referrals. Follow up with a phone call.

❏ Meet with other coaches and develop a coaching network. Occasionally coaches can't accommodate all their clients and need to refer some to another coach.

❏ Join with other local coaches to rent a booth or table at a local trade show or business expo.

❏ Sign up to assist with coach training courses, or to assist other coaches with their workshops.

❏ Send your clients greeting cards for their birthdays, unusual holidays (e.g., Valentine's Day, Fourth of July) or to congratulate them for a task well done.

❏ Send personal, hand written, thank you notes when anyone does you a favor. Don't miss an opportunity to establish a positive impression.

❏ Volunteer to be involved with activities in your local coaching organization.

❏ Volunteer to be involved in your local civic and service organizations (e.g., Rotary or SPCA).

❏ Serve on a board of directors for a local charity, association, or your local community college.

❏ Following a workshop or presentation, have the audience members put their business cards in a bowl for a drawing for a free month of coaching. After the event, send a personal thank-you note to each attendee.

❏ When introduced, even in a social setting, always mention that you are a coach. Be prepared with a 10 to 20 second description of the benefits of coaching.

❏ Make sure your clients, friends, family, and acquaintances know about coaching. Recruit them onto your informal marketing team!

❏ Offer a free sample session to anyone you talk with about coaching.

❏ Join a "leads club" such as LeTip, where people exchange contacts and referrals.

Create Unique and Varied Marketing Materials

❏ Develop a brochure and/or flier to hand out to potential clients or referral sources, or to display in locations where members of your niche can be found.

❏ Develop an elevator speech and use it.

❏ Invest in the best quality business cards, brochures, stationery, and web site you can afford.

❏ Collect interesting articles about coaching. Make copies and include them with your brochure. If you have a web site, obtain approval from the writer to put the article online as a reference.

❏ Create brochure inserts that are targeted toward your niche, e.g., technical writers or new mothers.

❏ Mail a lumpy envelope with your brochure. Lumpy envelopes get attention. You could mail a holiday ornament, seasonal decorations — whatever neat idea you come up with!

❏ Sign up for a coach referral service, available through ICF and some of the coaching schools.

❏ Publish your own newsletter.

❏ Write letters to the editor of your newspaper or a professional publication.

❏ Write articles for the ICF newsletter or your local paper.

❏ Create an informative and easy-to-use web site.

❏ Ask your clients for testimonials about your services. Put these on your brochure and web site.

❏ Purchase a directory listing and/or ad space in a directory targeted to one of your niches.

❏ Carry your business cards with you all the time. Always be ready to talk about coaching, its benefits, and your services.

❏ Have a professional photograph taken. Use it on your brochure and web site.

❏ Send a news release to your local newspaper when you have reached a milestone: e.g., certification, an award, in business for five years. These may be printed in the Business section.

❏ Send the same notice to your friends, family, colleagues and past clients.

❏ Create a radio ad and have it aired on a local radio station.

❏ Distribute information request cards at your seminars and workshops so attendees can request further information about coaching or some subject that you mention in your presentation. Follow-up with each request individually.

Display Your Talents

❏ Conduct free or low-cost workshops on living life in balance, goal setting, or other coaching-related topic.

❏ Speak at local service clubs such as Chamber of Commerce, Rotary, Lions, or Kiwanis. Some of these clubs meet weekly, and they are often seeking speakers.

❑ Do pro bono (i.e., free) coaching for non-profit organizations. Their managers typically welcome any assistance in juggling multiple priorities and staying focused.

❑ Donate a month of coaching to a fundraiser or silent auction for a charity, civic, or service organization. Typically your brochures and business cards will be displayed at the event, plus you'll get a short-term client.

❑ Make sure that your sample sessions are powerful and beneficial. Use an exercise that potential clients will find thought-provoking during and after the session.

❑ Offer a short course or seminar at your local community college, or adult education center.

❑ Be a volunteer coach at a local high school or college.

❑ Be a host or contributor to a local radio program.

Focus on You

❑ Become a certified coach, both through your coach training school and through ICF.

❑ Help your clients find a coach that works best for them. Don't hold onto a client who doesn't "fit" with you. Refer them to another trusted coach. The favor will be remembered and returned.

❑ Listen to what your potential clients say — every word. Make them feel that they have been heard, understood, and cherished.

❑ Take steps to ensure that your own life is in balance and fulfilling. "Walk the talk" by striving for your own dreams. Live the coaching life and show that you sincerely care about people.

12

Building
Your Brand

A good name is better than precious ointment.

ECCLESIASTES 7:1

E VERYTHING YOU PURCHASE — products and services — has a
brand. Look around you; they are everywhere. Levi's,
Starbucks, McDonalds, Maytag, The Gap, Toyota, Tide, South-
west Airlines, Nike, Bank of America, Roto-Rooter — these
are all examples of brands.

There are many elements that help reinforce a brand —
company name, product name, marketing materials, logos,
slogans, jingles — they all help strengthen a brand's clarity
and recognition. But the first step for all of them was the
development of a brand concept.

What Is a Brand?

A brand is a much broader concept than what we see as con-
sumers; it's more than just a name, a logo, and a slogan. In
their useful book "Be Your Own Brand," David McNally and
Karl Speak provide a widely accepted definition of a brand:

A brand is a perception or emotion, maintained by a buyer or a prospective buyer, describing the experience related to doing business with an organization or consuming its products or services.

This definition includes three notable points: a brand is an emotion or perception; your client or potential client experiences it; it's felt when your client or prospective client works or talks with you. In other words, your brand is how people feel or what they perceive when they are in relationship with you; the mental and emotional image they have of you during and after your interaction.

Strong brands begin when your clients/potential clients trust you, like you, remember you, value you, and relate to you. So how is a brand different from being a nice person? The added ingredient in a strong brand is the clear and consistent identification and communication of the qualities or characteristics that distinguish you from everyone else. You become memorable for a specific reason — for example, as a compassionate and powerful coach. Having a clear brand is a benefit for your clients because it helps them "classify" you in their mental Rolodex (another brand!), and it is a benefit for you because it further strengthens your image.

It's important to realize that we are subconsciously branded whenever we meet or talk with someone. Be honest. How many times have you met someone and had an emotional reaction or formed a perception or judgment? It happens *all* the time; it's part of being human. So why not use that to your advantage? Instead of letting chance decide how people feel about an interaction with you, take steps to positively shape their perceptions and feelings. That is the core of how a brand works — being consciously proactive about clearly and consistently communicating your uniqueness and value, and thereby influencing how you're perceived and remembered.

Developing Your Brand

There are several steps to developing a brand:

- Create an inventory of your unique characteristics relevant to your chosen niche
- From that list, select only those characteristics that represent your true essence
- With those essence words, create a branding statement that describes you, your services, and your value
- Implement your brand in your thoughts, actions, marketing materials, and business vision

"Oh my gosh," I can hear you thinking, "this sounds like a lot of work!" Actually, it's not, and I'm delighted to tell you that we've already discussed several topics that can help define your brand, such as your business vision (Chapter Two), how you want to be as a CEO (Chapter Three), your business plan (Chapter Four), your marketing self-assessment and your niche (both in Chapter Eleven). In each case, you were asked to look closely at yourself and determine the unique characteristics that set you apart from other coaches — your values, passions, personality traits, experiences, and areas of expertise, to name a few. You've done this groundwork already! In the workbook you'll find additional exercises that will walk you through the following steps.

The first step in developing your brand is a deep knowledge of yourself. Through your self-exploration, you will uncover many unique attributes that you might have taken for granted or not previously recognized.

The second step is to select only a few of those unique attributes to highlight in your business. Which ones represent the essence of who you are? Since we often don't see ourselves objectively, it can be helpful to get input and perspective from others who know you well or who know you as a coach — clients, significant other, family, colleagues, friends. Ask them to describe you in four to six words. What attributes do they see as your core characteristics? You will see patterns in the feedback that will point you toward your essence.

One tip is to focus only on those unique attributes that are relevant, or meaningful, to your niche. For example, an attribute that makes me unique is that I worked as a theatrical stage manager for a number of years. Even though this experience had a significant impact on me, it's not relevant to my niche of entrepreneurs and high achievers, so it's not one that I include in my brand. When you look at your list of unique attributes, focus first on those that you feel are both part of your essence and also relevant to your niche.

Now that you have eight to ten words that describe your essence, the next step is to craft your brand statement. How would you succinctly describe yourself and your value? For example, when I most recently went through these steps, the words that seemed to best describe my essence were: compassion, intelligence, experienced entrepreneur, clarity, calm, warmth, partnering, creativity, and humor. From these words, I developed my current branding statement: "I'm a seasoned entrepreneur and compassionate partner who brings clarity, humor, and creative intelligence to help calm the whirlwind of your life." Use the exercises in the workbook to help you develop your own branding words and statement. As with most aspects of your business, your branding words and statement will shift and change over time.

You'll know that you've reached your goal when you feel comfortable that the words and statement reflect who you are, how you want to be seen, and the value you bring to your clients. In addition, a successful brand has three key characteristics:

- It is relevant to the target audience (your niche)
- The brand message is clear and easy to grasp
- It is consistently communicated in a variety of ways

Putting Your Brand to Work

Now that you have branding words and a statement, what do you do with them? Lots of things! First, I recommend that you determine if your branding words and/or statement suggest any modifications for your business vision, business plan and goals, marketing self-assessment, or niche. All of these aspects of your business need to complement and support each other. They must be mutually consistent.

Next, there are three broad ways to implement and communicate your branding statement: in your heart and thoughts, in your words and behavior, and in your marketing materials. If your brand message is clear and consistent across these three categories, it will stand out clearly to your clients and potential clients.

In Your Heart and Thoughts

This is the most important place to implement your brand. If it isn't firmly rooted in your heart and your thoughts, it will not be effective. I don't mean merely memorized. Rather I mean that you should experience a feeling of truly owning the essence of the words and the statement.

Several times in this book we've discussed the power of our thoughts. What we think influences how we act and what we say; those influence how we are perceived; and that influences the reality of our lives. So it shouldn't be a surprise that putting your brand into action starts with your thoughts and how you see yourself. You need to truly *be* your brand.

When you start working with your branding statement, it may seem a little awkward to say, even to yourself. This is a normal reaction, so don't panic. You may want to start a daily routine of repeating your statement to yourself, and doing some journaling to explore what the branding words and statement mean to you. After a few weeks, it will become a natural part of your thoughts and your self-image.

Words and Behavior

With your branding words and statement in your heart and head, the words and behavior will naturally follow suit. However, talking about your brand may feel uncomfortable at first, so I suggest that you take additional time with your elevator speech (Chapter Thirteen) to ensure that your brand message comes through clearly. In addition, pay attention to your body language and your voice so that your natural warmth, confidence, and sincere interest in others aren't overshadowed by any nervousness you might feel.

The strongest perception your clients and potential clients will have about you will be based on your person-to-person interactions so the clarity and consistency of your brand message are very important.

Marketing Materials

Implementing your brand in your marketing materials is what differentiates a branding statement from a standard elevator speech. Your brand will be apparent in your words, behavior, and marketing materials. How cool is that?

When you begin work on your marketing materials (Chapter Thirteen), your branding statement and words will be a critical input. You will want to develop a visual theme that will support your brand message and be used consistently throughout your materials. This could include a logo, use of specific colors and graphics, a tag line, and consistent type font. Your graphic designer will have some helpful ideas.

Your Business Name

I've learned over the years that selecting a business name is one of the hardest decisions in starting a company. The name you choose will influence how clients perceive you. If it is hard to remember, too long, hard to pronounce, or confusing, it will not provide you with much benefit. But by choosing your company name wisely, it will strengthen your brand image and be a name that you'll be saying with pride and enjoyment.

Although naming a business is not easy, it can be fun. Don't be dismayed if you have a difficult time choosing a unique, descriptive name. The process takes time, creativity, an open mind, and some elbow grease. Above all, choose a name that you like! You'll be living with it for a long time.

Name Criteria

There are five important criteria to keep in mind while you are choosing the business name:

1. Be unique and memorable
2. Do not cause confusion with any existing name, trademark, or service mark
3. Project a professional image
4. Include a legal element if needed (Chapter Five)
5. Have an acceptable domain name available if desired (Chapter Sixteen)

In addition, if your practice is an S-Corporation or a Limited Liability Company (LLC), you must choose a name that will be acceptable to your Secretary of State. (Corporations and LLCs are discussed in Chapter Five.)

BE UNIQUE AND MEMORABLE

It's difficult to get people to remember company names, especially when the service is so closely linked to one person — you. Your current clients may not remember your business name, but they will remember your personal name. Nothing wrong with that! But potential clients — those people who don't yet know you — need to remember your business as well as you. So choose a business name that is distinctive and easy to remember. One way to facilitate memory is to choose a name that conveys something about the nature of the business. A name like "Kelley & Associates" tells you nothing about the company, which makes it harder to remember the name.

Revisit your branding words and statement, along with your business vision. Think about what type of image or feeling you want to convey with the business name. The exercises in the workbook will help you brainstorm, free associate, and play with potential names. Once your creative juices start to flow, many new ideas and words will pop into your head.

Do Not Cause Confusion with Existing Names, Trademarks, or Service Marks

According to Webster's Dictionary, "A trademark is a device, such as a symbol or name, that identifies a product, is officially registered, and is restricted by law to the exclusive use of the owner or manufacturer." Examples of trademarks include Camry automobiles and Dockers pants. A service mark has basically the same definition, but applied to the provider of a service, such as Roto-Rooter and Kinko's. A company name may be different than the trade or service mark; for example the Toyota Corporation (company name) sells cars under the Camry brand and trademark.

If your business name is too similar to an existing company name, trademark, or service mark, the owner of that trademark, service mark, or company name could start legal proceedings to stop you from using the name. You want to avoid this situation! This means that you will need to do some sleuthing to ensure that your name selection will not tread on anyone's toes. Here are some ways to research your potential business name:

- Do a search through your county's and/or state's fictitious business name files. The staff in your County Clerk or Recorder's office should be able to help you through this process.

- Look through business, trade, and local directories (such as the phone book, professional directories, Chamber of Commerce, and coach referral services). Some of these may be available at your local library in the reference section.
- Search for the name on the Internet, using as many search engines as possible. A list of well-known search engines is included in the companion workbook.
- Do a trademark search through the U.S. Patent and Trademark Office (USPTO) at www.uspto.gov, using their online TESS system.

If or when you file to become an LLC or S-Corporation, your Secretary of State will check to ensure that your business name is not a duplicate or similar to others in their files. But that office does not check any other resource. Approval from the state filing office is not a guarantee that your business name is not infringing on the legal rights of another party. So make sure to do your own research.

KEEP IT PROFESSIONAL

It's stating the obvious, but you want to project a professional image with your business name. Think about the business name from your potential clients' perspectives. What words would make them more interested in your coaching services and more likely to call?

Words or terms that could be inflammatory, offensive, or inappropriate should be avoided. Business names that sound cute now may not remain cute. Your business name should neither suggest that you are part of the government nor should it falsely describe your company. Therefore, company names like "Solve All Your Problems Coaching," or "Get Free Money Here Coaching," or "U.S. Department of Coaching" are names to leave *off* of your brainstorm list.

Business names also say something about the size of a company. Although the use of one's initials or surname in the business name does decrease the chance of a trademark issue, it does not project the image of a large firm. A name like "Kelley's Coaching" implies a one-person firm. This is not a bad thing, but it's wise to consider this perception before you decide on your business name.

INCLUDE A LEGAL ELEMENT

Each state has laws about what needs to be included in an LLC or corporation business name. The Secretary of State can provide you with an information packet when you start the application process. Typical legal terms that denote the type of business entity are Incorporated (Inc.), Corporation (Corp.), or Limited Liability Company (LLC). These business structures are discussed further in Chapter Five.

HAVE AN AVAILABLE DOMAIN NAME

The explosion of the Internet as both a communication and marketing tool has added a new wrinkle into the business name selection process. The purpose of a domain name is to provide your business with a unique Internet address. You are already familiar with many domain names such as yahoo.com and amazon.com.

If you plan to have a web site, or a unique email address, then you will need to research potential domain names. The most comprehensive way to research a domain name is to utilize a domain name registration web sites (two well-known sites are www.networksolutions.com and www.register.com). At these sites you will be able to research which domain names are taken, and the sites also include functionality to help you construct a domain name.

Domain name registration is discussed further in Chapter Sixteen. For now, just focus on the research step to determine if your desired domain name is available.

Potential Naming Techniques

GEOGRAPHIC NAMES

A business name can use the name of your city, county, region, street, or neighborhood without running into any ownership conflicts. No one can own place names. This type of name can be limiting if the location name is well recognized, for example, San Francisco Coaching. But Shadow Brook Coaching or Gabilan Coaching are less constraining because they are less recognizable, but may also be less memorable. Consider also the potential impact if you move, for example Monterey Bay Coaching with a business address of Tucson, Arizona.

DESCRIPTIVE NAMES

A truly descriptive name can be difficult to create if the service you provide is hard to succinctly describe, which can be the case with coaching. However, the use of key words, phrases, or terms that are applicable and/or associated with coaching may provide good name opportunities.

Don't limit yourself to English words only; check out words in foreign languages. Good resources include a foreign language dictionary and a thesaurus.

Words that have absolutely no relationship to coaching can also be used, as in Apple Coaching. But often they are harder to remember without somehow tying the name to the business, either through the story of the name's significance, or through frequent use in advertising.

SURNAMES

This popular technique simplifies the naming process, but does have a disadvantage. As mentioned earlier, using your initials or your surname can project a lone-wolf image. However, if you are in a coaching partnership you can use multiple surnames.

CREATED NAMES

These are names that you make up, through a combination of words, parts of words, or sounds. This type of name has increased in popularity, as there is no baggage associated with the definition of the word. Plus, these names can be used in any type of business. They are unique, distinct, and have little risk of trademark or name infringement. However, it takes time and energy to create this type of name, and they can be more difficult to remember. Well-known examples of created names (and brands) are Kodak and Tupperware.

13

Marketing Materials

Plans are only good intentions unless
they immediately degenerate into hard work.

PETER DRUCKER

YOU ARE YOUR MOST VALUABLE marketing asset — your personality, your background and experiences, your ability to establish rapport and connect with clients. All other marketing materials — brochures, web sites, business cards — are just secondary backups to you; they complement and assist you but they do not replace you. These materials may pique someone's interest or provide additional information, but it is very rare that someone will hire you as a coach based solely on your marketing materials. So *you* are the most important, and the most visible, part of your marketing materials.

Each time you meet a prospective client, impressions are formed based on how you appear, how you act, and what materials you provide. Your marketing materials, though few in number, need to reinforce the professional image, coaching message, and brand that you want to convey.

However, don't think that you have to wait until all your marketing materials are compete before you can start networking and talking with people. Start that right away! Develop and introduce your marketing materials as your time and funds allow.

In this chapter we will look at six fundamental marketing materials. These are listed below in the recommended order of development.

1. Elevator speech
2. Business card and company logo
3. Brochure
4. Introductory letters
5. Information sheets and fliers
6. Web site

Here are some tips and suggestions that are useful for all types of marketing materials.

- Reacquaint yourself with the work you've done to define the business image you want to project (Chapters Two, Three, Eleven, and Twelve). In addition, review your self-assessment and niche definition from Chapter Eleven. Your vision, brand, desired business image, special attributes, and target niches are all key inputs into the design of your marketing materials.
- These materials are the visual and/or physical components of your brand. Try to keep a common theme or feeling. The repeated use of graphics, slogans, layout formats, tone of speech, and general look and feel will help create consistency and a stronger brand message.
- For marketing materials that are text-intensive, such as brochures, introductory letters, and web sites, have them edited by an experienced writer or editor, or at least someone with "fresh eyes" and a good command of the language. An editor will add polish to your text as well as find any typos or grammatical errors.

- Try out your designs on colleagues, friends, and family members before you finalize the product. Does the piece have the intended impact? Is it clear and informative? Does it look appealing? Is anything missing?
- It's wise to copyright your marketing materials, especially your brochure and web site. A copyright will protect your materials from being copied and used by someone else. To claim a copyright, all that is needed is "Copyright *Year* by *Your Name*" somewhere on the document. An example is "Copyright 2003 by Dorcas Kelley."
- Most importantly, don't get stuck trying to make the "perfect" product. It doesn't exist! The goal is to develop a good (not perfect) product, use it, get feedback, watch for reactions, and then make adjustments as needed. Your marketing materials will change over time.
- Remember that you are your main marketing asset. Your marketing materials are there to support you, not to take your place. If you get too focused on the materials, you won't have the time, energy, or motivation to get out and do the direct marketing activities that are vital to the success of your practice.

Elevator Speech

Imagine that you're in an elevator with a potential client. You need to describe the value of coaching, your services, and your unique attributes in the ten seconds it takes to get from the ground floor to your destination floor. This is an elevator speech, and is one of the most useful marketing materials to have. In addition - it's free! Here are some development guidelines:

- Keep it short and concise. Less than 15-seconds long, only three or four sentences.

- Incorporate your branding words and statement.
- Make sure it's clear what you do and what the benefits are, for example:
  - What is coaching? Why would someone want a coach?
  - What are the benefits that coaching could provide to this individual?
  - What are your special attributes or skills that you bring to coaching?

Here is an example elevator speech:

"Hi, my name is Dorcas Kelley and I'm a business and personal coach. I help entrepreneurs and high achievers overcome obstacles and reach their goals. Through coaching, you can become more focused, more productive, and more fulfilled in your life and work. I've worked in high tech as a consultant and a coach for over fifteen years, so I understand the challenges you face in this industry."

Have multiple variations of your speech so you can quickly adapt to your audience (e.g., are they a part of the high tech industry or some other niche?) and available time (e.g., is this a quick how-do-you-do or a more lengthy introduction?).

Refine and practice your elevator speeches so you can recite them naturally and easily. Use the speech (or a part of it) when you are being introduced to others. It helps people know something about you and also segues easily into a discussion about coaching and your practice. Think of it as a quick advertisement for your business!

If you want to improve your communication and speaking skills, consider joining your local chapter of Toastmasters (www.toastmasters.org) or Speaking Circles (www.speakingcircles.com). This will help your coaching too!

Business Card and Logo

A business card with a logo is one of the least expensive and highest impact marketing materials you can have. Business cards are a level playing field — all businesses have them, from Fortune 50s to Mom & Pops — and there is a limited number of expensive bells and whistles. They don't have to be expensive, fancy, or have complicated graphics. Your logo can be as simple as your business name in a good typeface and color. A graphical component to the logo will make it more distinctive and professional, but it's not required.

Investing in a high quality business card and logo is worth the expense, as it is a relatively low cost way to look professional, strengthen your brand message, and provide some information about your practice. Any added creativity or uniqueness in the card and logo design will distinguish both you and your business. There are several alternatives for designing and printing your card and logo:

- You can hire a graphic designer to create the design and layout, or you can do the design work yourself.
- You can have the cards professionally printed, or you can print them yourself.

A professionally designed and printed card will look more polished and professional, and will be of higher quality. The cost for these services can vary from $100 to $2,500 and can take two to eight weeks from start of design to receiving the finished cards (depending on design complexity and number of revisions). In general, there are four steps to design and print business cards and logos:

1. Design advance work
2. Creating the design and layout
3. Final review and approval
4. Printing

Design Advance Work

It will save you money, time, and effort if you do some design advance work before talking with the designer or sitting down to create your own design. Going to a design meeting without any ideas about what you want and don't want means that the design process will start from scratch. Your costs will then include the time it takes for the designer to learn about your business, the image you want to convey, and your own personal likes and dislikes. Since you are the best source for all this information, it is more efficient to develop some ideas before you start the clock ticking.

The objective of the advance work is for you to develop preliminary ideas about logos and business card layouts that you like and that might work for your business. Included in the workbook is a number of quick, simple steps you can take to help you in this process.

When you begin discussions with the graphic designer, bring in your notes, sketches, copies, and ideas. The designer will be pleased that you've done the advance work, and your wallet will thank you as well.

Graphic Designers

Professional card layout and logo designs can cost anywhere from $100 to $2,500 or more. There are many graphic designers out there, and a positive recommendation should steer you to a good one. The best sources for a recommendation are colleagues, friends, and clients. Another source is to ask someone whose business card or logo you like. Other sources include local printers, your local Chamber of Commerce, or the Yellow Pages.

Always ask to see samples of the designer's previous work. Keep looking until you find a designer that you are comfortable with, does good quality work within your budget, and has a design style that fits with your ideas. Ask for three customer references and call at least one of those. Ask the reference about the designer's work style, attention to detail, and whether the work was performed within budget and on time.

Graphic design work can be done remotely, so don't limit your search to just your local area. Phone calls and email can easily replace the face-to-face meetings and approval steps. Drafts of the business card and logo design can be faxed, sent as email attachments, or with an express service such as FedEx.

The Design Process

The design process is iterative, meaning that you will receive rough sketches or ideas from the designer, and you will need to provide feedback that the designer can then incorporate into the next set of sketches.

You may get a card layout and logo designed right away, or it may take several iterations. You want to be really comfortable with the design *before* the print job is submitted. The workbook contains a number of tips to help the design and printing process go smoothly.

Business Card Printing

Once you have approved the design, your graphic designer will provide you with a set of printing instructions, a color printout of the design (so you can show the printer what the cards look like) plus a soft copy of the files on diskette.

The next step is to submit the print job. If you get your cards professionally printed, there is a wide range of paper quality. The paper's thickness, color, and weave (texture) all impact the perception of the card. Don't just take the recommendation of your designer or printer. Look at other paper selections as well and make sure that the combination of the paper and the design works for you.

If you want to print the cards yourself, there are several sources of business card stock, which typically has 10 blank business cards per sheet. These sheets can be fed through your laser jet or ink jet printer and each card has perforated edges for easy separation. The stock might be blank white, or might have a design.

There are two drawbacks to using these cards: They are made of thinner paper than printed business cards and so do not have the same look and feel, and they have the tell-tale perforated edge (which can be cut off with a paper cutter). Both of these characteristics negatively impact the professional image of your business cards.

However, they also have three advantages: they are less expensive, you can print only the number you need, and you can change the design at any time.

Brochures

Research has shown that humans do not adapt quickly or easily to change. Since coaching is a relatively new profession, it represents a change to most people's mindset about the helping professions. Historically, a person would seek help from a counselor, psychologist, or psychiatrist only if there was something *wrong*. The idea that someone might be creative, resourceful, and whole, *and* have a coach can represent a significant change in perspective.

A brochure facilitates this change in perspective as well as providing important information about your coaching practice. Here are some additional reasons why a brochure can be a valuable marketing tool:

- It provides a written description of your services, which is beneficial since humans typically need to hear and read the same piece of information several times before it really sinks in.
- It gives the prospective client a chance to read about coaching, its benefits, your services, and your background without you being physically present.
- It gives you a forum in which to provide critical infor-

mation about coaching benefits, client testimonials, your branding message and other information that may not be requested or appropriate during your discussion.
- If done well, a brochure will enhance the perception of professionalism and credibility.

Before you develop a brochure, make sure you have answered the following questions:

- Who is your target audience?
- What will the reader learn from your brochure? What is the brochure's objective?
- How will the reader get your brochure? How will you distribute it?

Having your brochures professionally printed looks really nice, but often is expensive. However, the new technology of professional digital presses can substantially reduce the cost, even for small batches. If you decide to get your brochures professionally printed, make sure to ask your printer if they have access to this newer technology.

Another alternative is to print them yourself on your laser or ink-jet printer. There are several mail order paper companies that offer a wide selection of pre-folded patterned papers at a reasonable cost. You can print just the number of brochures that you need, and can easily modify the text and layout. (A selection of companies is listed in the workbook.)

If you have your brochure design done by a professional, make sure to get a copy of the file so you can modify it yourself when needed.

Brochures are meant to be informative, but not overwhelming. Keep this in mind during the design process. In the workbook you will find several worksheets to help you design your brochure, as well as tips for the printing process.

Introductory Letters

Introductory letters are useful when you are doing a brochure mailing, or when you are notifying your friends, relatives, and colleagues of your coaching business. Many of the points already discussed are applicable for introductory letters. Here are a few additional tips:

- Be clear about the objective of the letter — what are the two or three main points that you want to make?
- Develop an outline for the letter before you start to write, and incorporate your main points.
- The letter should be no more than one page long, and the page should have plenty of white space on it.
- For visual interest, use bullet points for lists (such as coaching benefits), or use questions to involve the reader ("Are you enjoying your life to the fullest?")
- Touch upon more personal subjects such as why you became a coach or what kind of people you enjoy working with. Write the letter in the first person, for example "I'm really excited to tell you that ...."
- Use everyday language and avoid coach terminology.
- Have your letter reviewed by a professional editor.
- Have an opening paragraph that is engaging and grabs your reader's attention. Universally recognized situations ("Have you ever ...") and humor are great ways to start.
- Your letter should be independent of the brochure. Don't refer to the brochure except to note "Enclosed is my brochure to provide additional information."
- Offer something of value to the reader — an exercise, an inquiry, a quick self-quiz (with answers or some type of explanation), plus an offer for a free sample session. Or, enclose a gift certificate for a sample session that the reader could give to a friend or colleague.
- Include an article about coaching. This adds to the credibility of coaching, provides additional information, and

also provides value to the reader.
- Use nice stationery (including the envelope) that complements or coordinates with the brochure.
- Say that you will follow up and then do it! Don't wait for the recipient to contact you. You may want to send out the brochures in small batches (about ten at a time), so you aren't faced with a long list of phone calls to make in a short period of time.

Fliers and Information Sheets

Like brochures, fliers and information sheets should be developed when there is a clear need, typically to announce a workshop, presentation, or special event. First, determine the key information: Who will read the flier? How will they receive it? What do you want them to learn from the document? There are typically five main elements to a flier:

- Headline
- Description of the event and the benefits to the attendees
- Logistical information — when, where, cost (if any)
- Brief presenter biography
- Contact information to get more details — phone number, email address, web address

Fliers can be printed on colored paper, or on the pre-printed papers sold by mail order companies. The pre-printed papers look more professional and polished, but the colored paper is more easily available and less expensive.

Business Web Site

The final piece of marketing material is your business web site. There are several benefits to having a web site:

- It serves as an online, easy to access, relatively easy to update brochure. When someone says "Can you send me some information about your coaching services?" you can give them your web address. This greatly simplifies the contact process with remote prospects, since you won't have to mail them anything.
- It shows to potential clients that your business is legitimate. No matter how professional your image, clients will still have some amount of trepidation about hiring a relatively unknown person in a relatively new field. Having a well-organized and informative web site will put these concerns to rest.
- It can include a vast amount of information and resources. You can post reference materials (such as articles and links to other web sites), self-assessment surveys, exercises, and newsletters. The options are nearly endless. There is no other media that allows so much flexibility to include such a variety of items.

Web sites come in all shapes and sizes, from a simple one-page design to an interactive catalog and shopping site. When thinking about your first web site, heed the advice of experts: start small and simple. Your site will grow and develop over time so your initial version should be done relatively quickly and with a limited amount of expense.

In the remainder of this chapter, and in the workbook, we'll cover some tips for finding a web site developer, design advance work to complete before development begins, some guidelines for web site design, and how to list your web site with Internet search engines.

Finding a Web Site Developer

You may want to hire a professional to do the initial web site development or you may want to try your hand at it. The development process is not complex but it does take time to learn a web development program and the technology to upload and maintain a web site. Whether you do it yourself or hire it out is dependent on the time you have available and your inclination to learn the software and related technology.

There are an abundance of web developers, so how do you find a good one who fits your style and budget? First, ask colleagues, friends, and business acquaintances for recommendations. Also ask your Internet service provider and web hosting service (discussed in Chapter Sixteen). They may be able to recommend a developer they have worked with, and may have developers on staff or on contract. Another option is to "cruise the net" and find web sites that you like. Typically the web developer's name and/or company will be listed somewhere on the home page along with a link to send them an email. Other options include asking your local Chamber of Commerce, or looking in the Yellow Pages (both the printed and Internet versions).

When you find a potential developer, ask for the web addresses of previous work. As with graphic designers, you need to find a developer who matches your personal style. Keep looking until you find one you are comfortable with, who does good quality work within your budget, and who has a design style that works for your company image. Ask for three customer references, and call at least one of those. Ask the reference about the developer's work style, attention to detail, and whether the work was performed within budget and on time.

Web development can be done remotely, so don't limit your search to just your local area. Phone calls and email can easily replace the face-to-face meetings and approval steps. Drafts of the web pages can be sent as email attachments and previewed with your web browser.

Design Advance Work

Similar to the logo and business card design process, it will save you time, money, and effort if you do some advance work before talking with the developer. Advantages to documenting some ideas concerning the content, organization, and desired look and feel of the web site prior to finding a developer include:

- You will have a better sense of your desired design style.
- You will be able to provide better guidance to the potential developer. This will allow the developer to give you a more accurate quote both for cost and for development time frame.
- You will minimize the overall development cycle time as neither you nor the developer will be starting from a blank page.

The objective of this advance work is for you to develop a rough idea, or vision, of how the web site should look and what it should contain. In addition, you will be creating the text or content for each of the pages included in your web site. In the workbook you will find a recommended process to complete the advance work.

Web Site Design and Development

With your advance work complete, you are ready to kick off the design and development efforts. Send your developer copies of your web site mockups and review them together.

Web site development is iterative. You will see drafts of the design via email attachments (using your web browser), or by logging onto the developer's web site. You will then provide feedback to the developer that will be incorporated into the next set of drafts. The development process can take anywhere from two weeks to six months, depending on the complexity of the design and the number of iterations.

Although you may not be directly creating the web site, you will be responsible for providing feedback and approving the design. With this in mind, it's important to have an idea of what design features can make a web site more or less effective. The workbook contains a number of tips for good web site design.

When your web site is complete, your developer should upload it onto your web hosting service and into your domain name. Your web site will then be "live." If you are developing your own web site, contact your web host to get the proper upload instructions.

Search Engines

Now that your web site is live, you'll want to get some traffic to check it out! Ideally within those users will be some prospective clients. But first, they have to find your site.

Each year, Georgia Tech University conducts a survey (The GVU WWW User Survey) on computer and Internet use. The most recent survey found that 85% of Internet users found sites by using search engines. Links from other websites was the first ranked source at 88%. The third and fourth slots were 65% for friends/word of mouth and 63% for printed media. Clearly, getting registered on search engines is a fundamental way to increase your site's traffic.

I use the term "search engine" as a generic term to include both true search engines and also directories. The difference between these two is how the listings are compiled. True search engines use "robots" or "spiders" to automatically "crawl" through the Internet, examining and indexing web site contents. In contrast, directories rely on humans to do the crawling and indexing.

Currently, leading true search engines include Google, FAST, and Inktomi. The most widely known directory is Yahoo!, along with LookSmart and The Open Directory. Surprised that you don't recognize many of these names? That's because many search engines we use on the Internet are powered by another company's technology. For example, MSN Search is powered by Inktomi and AOL Search uses Google.

Using search engines as an effective marketing tool requires two steps:

1. Search engine submission or registration
2. Optimizing your listing

SEARCH ENGINE SUBMISSION

The first step is to get the search engines to notice your site! There are several ways to accomplish this:

- You can do nothing and wait until the true search engine robots find your site. Given the proliferation of web sites, this alternative can take up to nine months. But it's free and requires you to do nothing.
- You can contact the leading search engines and proactively tell them about your site. This is called submitting or registering your web site. Some search engines offer this service for free, others charge a one-time fee. This will speed up the process and you might see your listing in one to three months.
- You can purchase a paid listing in a search engine, which is the fastest way to get listed and typically assures you of a top placement. This is the most expensive option, and you pay either a monthly fee or on a pay-per-click basis.
- Finally, you can register with a search engine registration service. These services will register your site with hundreds of search engines. Some services charge a one-time fee, others are on an annual basis. Make sure you select a service that will register you with the mainstream search engines, such as Google, FAST, Inktomi, Yahoo, LookSmart, and Teoma.

Whatever alternative you choose, when the search engines do notice you, your web site will be reviewed and categorized based on words or phrases that are repeated on your web pages. So, if you want to be listed under "spiritual coaching" in a search engine, make sure that this phrase is used (several times, if possible) in your web site.

Typically, once you are found by one search engine, you will quickly be found by others. That is because search engines search each other, as well as searching through the whole Internet.

As a search engine, Yahoo! is a category by itself. Yahoo! is currently the most popular directory on the Internet, and it is very different than all other search engines. Getting a listing on Yahoo! is notoriously difficult to do. Yahoo! editors review hundreds of sites each day and reject up to 90% of them. They look for high quality web sites that offer something unique and of value. Here are some tips specific to getting a listing on Yahoo!:

- The web site content must provide value and benefit. The editors look for useful sites with worthwhile information. They are biased towards information rather than products.
- Quality design is a must. This includes the page layout, how quickly it loads and its overall look and feel.
- Size does matter. The Yahoo! editors are more likely to reject a one-page site than a multi-page site.

OPTIMIZING YOUR LISTING

So now your web site is listed in some search engines. That's great, and it's not enough, because your web site might be listed last within a category, and that won't bring you much traffic. Therefore, it's important to prepare your web site so that it is focused in ways that will improve the chances that your site will be found. Although there is no "silver bullet" to improving your listing location, there are three main tips to be aware of while you are designing your site.

The first tip is *Location*. Using the earlier example, the term "spiritual coaching" should be used toward the top of your home page and other connecting pages, either in the page headline or in the first few paragraphs on the page. In addition, the phrase should be listed in the home page's HTML Title Meta Tag (ask your developer for details).

A second tip is *Frequency.* The more you use that phrase in your web site, the greater the chances for a higher listing. This does not mean filling up a whole page with nothing but "spiritual coaching" repeated over and over — that type of behavior would most likely get your web site banned from search engines altogether.

The third tip is *Connection.* What other sites are linked to yours? The content of those sites will help the search engine classify you. For example, a link to the ICF web site would be better for a coach than a link to Bill's Hardware Store. The number of links will help you as well.

Although following these tips won't guarantee you a high placement in a search engine, it will improve the probability. Keep in mind that each search engine is built differently, so great results in one search engine won't necessarily translate to other listings.

An excellent resource that provides broader and deeper information about search engines — how they work, what they are, how to optimize listings, which ones to contact — can be found at http://www.searchenginewatch.com.

14

Effective Networking

*Fear makes strangers of people
who should be friends.*

SHIRLEY MACLAINE

COACHING IS A RELATIONSHIP BUSINESS. You won't be hired unless your prospective client feels some level of trust and rapport with you. Although your marketing materials will discuss what you do and a little about who you are, the decision to hire you as a coach will depend on how you relate to that person.

So how do these relationships start? You already have relationships with prospective clients or referral sources. Look at your current sphere of influence — your friends, colleagues, acquaintances, neighbors, and family. Don't underestimate the value these individuals can bring to your business. Tell them about your passion for coaching and your special skills and attributes. Offer them a sample session and request their assistance in referring your services to others. Follow up with a hand written thank you note for their time and support.

Of course, there are a lot of people you haven't met yet, and that is where networking is a vital skill. Networking is one of the least expensive and most powerful marketing activities. It can happen almost anytime, anywhere — at volunteer events, charity fundraisers, sporting events, churches, community presentations, schools, cultural events, and even neighborhood parties.

It's important to have the perspective that networking is an investment in the future. Don't expect to go to one networking event and come home with scores of new clients. Successful networking takes consistent presence at the various events, patience, and a methodical process. The remainder of this chapter will describe an effective networking method.

Finding the Venues

Networking venues are the places you will go to meet people. Each community is different, so look up "Associations," "Social Service Organizations," and "Professional Organizations" in the Yellow Pages. Read through the business and community sections of your local newspaper for upcoming events and presentations. Call your local Chamber of Commerce and ask about their networking events. Ask your family, friends, and colleagues for recommendations. Your city might have a web site with a calendar of upcoming events. Appropriate venues can also include social clubs, dog parks, soccer fields, where ever you might meet members of your niche. You will probably find that there are many more networking opportunities than you had imagined.

While keeping in mind your target niche, choose one to three initial venues. The organizations you select could be all business-related, or a mixture of civic, social, general business, and professional. Select whatever mixture you feel will provide the best opportunity to meet potential clients in your niche market. Be prepared to attend the meetings for at least three months to see if there is a "fit" between your needs and the organization and/or location.

Event Preparation

With the upcoming meetings noted on your calendar, you now need to prepare. Here are five preparation steps:

1. Have your business cards ready to go and plan to take at least 15 of them.

2. Review your elevator speech(es). One question you will be asked is "What do you do?" If necessary, modify your elevator speech so that it flows smoothly from that question. Also develop a longer elevator speech (up to 30 seconds) in case the networking event has an introduction period where the attendees introduce themselves and briefly speak about their business. Rehearse so you feel comfortable with your speeches.

3. Another question you will be asked is "What is coaching?" This question presents a challenge since coaching is both a new field and one that can be difficult to describe. Don't try to explain *about* coaching or compare it to another field (such as therapy), or discuss the coaching process. Focus instead on describing the outcomes or results from coaching. Here are some examples:
    *   Coaching is where clients work to define and achieve their life goals.
    *   Through coaching, clients clarify their values and develop a roadmap to a more balanced life.
    *   I'm a coach who works with small business owners to help them achieve personal and professional success.
    *   I'm a coach who challenges my clients to charge after their dreams.
    *   Coaching is like having a personal life trainer.
    *   Coaching is like having someone to challenge your growth in life.

4. When you rehearse, pay attention to your voice and body language to make sure they match your words. People absorb and process body language and voice tone much faster than words. For example, if you are talking about how energizing coaching is, but your body is tense and your voice is meek, the impression will be that you are definitely *not* energized. The body language message is always perceived more quickly than your words, and will remain in the listener's memory much longer than anything you might say. If there is a conflict between your words and your behavior, your listener will believe your behavior, not your words. If you want to improve your communication and speaking skills, consider joining a local chapter of Toastmasters (www.toastmasters.org) or Speaking Circles (www.speakingcircles.com).

5. Prepare some powerful questions that you might ask people during the networking event. Remember that you'll be talking with people about their businesses, jobs, lives, and the associated challenges and accomplishments. Some appropriate powerful coaching questions might be:
   * What would you like to be doing in five years?
   * If you could do that over again, what would you do differently?
   * If you could do anything you wanted, what would you do?
   * What's stopping you?
   * What was the lesson from that experience?
   * Where will that action lead you?

Once you've gotten your business cards, rehearsed your introduction and powerful questions, and paid attention to your body language, you're all set to hit the networking circuit!

Attending Events

So, you're in your nice clothes at the door of the networking event. Now what?

Some people believe that networking is just talking with as many people as possible and handing out business cards. They are wrong. Those folks aren't really networking but promoting themselves, which is typically a one-way discussion that isn't very engaging.

Nearly everyone feels anxious at the prospect of mingling in a room full of strangers. It's natural to feel nervous, but try to not let your discomfort constrain your activities. Start slowly until you feel more comfortable with the situation. You'll find that as you meet people and attend events, the nervousness will decrease.

So what *should* you do? Here are some tips.

- At most networking events, it is assumed that new people join in at each event. So walk through the door, find someone who looks interesting and introduce yourself. "Hi, I'm Dorcas Kelley and this is the first time I've attended this meeting. What's your name?" After the introductions, you might ask "What type of work do you do?" and the conversation will unfold from there.
- The good news is that with your skills of listening and asking powerful questions, you just need to attend these events with a coach perspective. That's right — just show up and listen, be curious, be interested, ask powerful questions, empathize, and clarify or mirror their statements. Being an engaged and friendly conversation partner is the biggest success factor in effective networking.
- As you interact with people, remember three things:
  1. Listen and ask questions more than you speak.
  2. It's not the quantity of people you meet, but the quality of your interactions. It is much more effective to leave with two business cards from people with whom

you had a good conversation rather than 20 cards from people with whom you barely spoke.

3. By showing sincere interest you become more engaging to your conversation partners. They in turn will become more interested in you and your coaching practice. In addition, they will be more open to what you say because you have taken the time to really listen to them.

- The less comforting news is that you will need to talk about yourself, your coaching practice, and the benefits of coaching. But you've rehearsed your elevator speech and your description of coaching, so you are well prepared! Try to relax and be natural, even if you feel nervous.

- During a conversation, determine if there is something of value that you can offer to the other person, for example an article that addresses a subject she's discussing or a business contact that she might find useful. If you think of something, offer to send it to her. Once you trade business cards, write down what you promised her so you won't forget. It's also a good memory jogger to write down some detail about her, such as her job, company, special interests, or the topics you discussed.

- Don't worry if you don't have anything of value to offer. Get her business card anyway. It's an expected exchange at a networking event. Just ask, "Do you have a business card with you?" and make sure to offer one of yours in return. On the back of the card, jot down some subjects that the two of you discussed, as well as some details about her.

- If someone seems interested in learning more about coaching, offer them a free sample session. Tell them that you will call the following day to set up a convenient time.

- A final tip is to come early to networking events and

leave late. This practice will give you plenty of time to have good conversations with two to four people, depending on the length of the event. Being "fashionably late" will just reduce your available networking time.

After the Event

For the people who don't know how to network effectively, the end of the event is just that — the end. But to make your networking time really pay off, it's the follow-up *after* the event that will solidify your relationships with the people you've met.

- The following day, send off the articles, references, and contact names that you promised. But don't just send an impersonal email with the information. Instead, send a hand-written note. Mention your enjoyment of the conversation and that you are enclosing the information you had promised to send. Also send one of your brochures to provide more information on your practice. Follow up again with the person in a week's time to make sure they got the information and to find out if you can be of any further assistance.
- Follow up by phone with the people who requested a sample session. Mail them a brochure with a copy of a coaching-related article. Once the sample session is complete, a hand-written thank-you note should be sent, followed a week later by a phone call to ask if they found the session useful and if they know of anyone who might be interested in your services.
- Send thank-you notes to your other networking contacts, expressing your pleasure at having met them and mentioning some topic that the two of you discussed. Send a brochure as well.
- The notes you write need to be sincere. Only send notes

to those individuals with whom you would like a networking relationship. Add those people to your distribution list for notices, newsletters, or similar information.

- As time goes by, keep an eye out for items that would be of value to the people you have met at the networking events. Sending articles, web site addresses, contact names, even cartoons are a great way to stay in touch. Each time you send something, follow up by phone about one week later to find out if the information was useful and to answer any related questions.

- If the person calls to thank you, ask them out for lunch or coffee. Even if the person doesn't call back to thank you, call and ask them out anyway. Tell them that you'd like to learn more about what they do, and would also like to get their advice about what you do.

- Regardless of what organizations you join, the best way to get the most out of your membership is to get involved and become more visible. Volunteer to make a presentation, work on a committee, donate a month of coaching for a silent auction, be a project manager for an upcoming charitable event, become a board member — whatever is needed. The more involved you are, the more visible you will be and the more the members of the organization will know about you and your business.

Effective networking takes more time than just attending the events. But the investment in time and effort is well worth the payoff. Not only will you gain clients, you'll also gain a solid network of supporters and referral sources.

Around the Office

We lift ourselves by our thought, we climb upon our vision of ourselves. If you want to enlarge your life, you must first enlarge your thought of it and of yourself. Hold the ideal of yourself as you long to be, always, everywhere - your ideal of what you long to attain - the ideal of health, efficiency, success.

ORISON SWETT MARDEN

THE TOPICS COVERED SO FAR have touched upon many subjects but not the most personal ones — your day-to-day business life and your work environment. Of all the topics in this book, these are the most pervasive and intimate because they touch your life every workday.

Becoming self-employed is a big step. There is no company or management hierarchy to dictate a work schedule, priorities, deadlines, goals, equipment, and performance evaluations. It's all up to you. How marvelous, and also how intimidating.

In this section we'll focus on three key topics: your transition into self-employment, your contact methods (e.g., mail, email, phone, fax), and your physical office space and equipment.

15

The Transition to Self-Employment

If you can DREAM it, you can DO it.

WALT DISNEY

WHILE IT'S WONDERFUL that you no longer have someone else telling you what to do and when and how to do it, that role doesn't disappear — it just transfers onto your shoulders. You are now the boss *and* the employee. You are responsible for structuring your workday and environment, and defining what are acceptable and unacceptable results.

It's so enjoyable to take the day off, watch an old movie, take your child to the park, organize a closet, or sign up for a midday yoga class. It's so tempting to do all those activities that you never could get to while you were working a corporate job. Is it possible to enjoy these activities and still get your work done? Yes, it is. But it may require that you develop some new skills and a new perspective about work.

Self-employment is both heaven and hell. On one hand are the heavenly advantages of setting your own schedule and the flexibility to do what you want when you want and the way you want. On the other hand are the potentially hellish and intimidating responsibilities of self-organization, self-discipline, and self-motivation.

This can seem like an overwhelming responsibility, but it doesn't need to be! You are entirely capable of setting goals, establishing priorities, managing time, being efficient, and warding off the demon of procrastination. As a coach, you often work with your clients on these same issues!

What you need is a system, or process, to help you manage your time efficiently and effectively. With a system that is designed around your goals, values, preferences, and needs, you can handle both your work and your other responsibilities without total exhaustion. In addition to a process, you need a support network to help motivate you and hold you accountable.

The Structure of Work

When you were employed by another company, your day was in large part structured by your work. You got up in the morning, got dressed, had a bite to eat, and commuted to work. At work you had tasks to complete and projects to work on. There were managers to establish the priorities and departmental goals to reach. When your workday was done, you headed out the door and commuted back home where your evening was filled with family, friends, and other obligations.

Shouldn't the transition to self-employment be easier, since you can do whatever you want? The answer is both yes and no. Yes, because you now have the *flexibility* to establish your own schedule based on what you want. No, because you now have the *responsibility* to establish your own schedule and goals. Most of us have little or no experience at running our own lives however we want. It's probably a new skill for you to learn.

By leaving the other company, you lost the structure that your work provided. For example, in most jobs:

- There are expectations regarding the length of the work-week and the workday, with general rules regarding starting and ending times, lunch and coffee breaks.
- There are company and department goals articulated for the month, the quarter, and the year.
- You have to physically go to the work site. Working every day at home in your bathrobe is probably not an option.
- There are expectations regarding acceptable and unacceptable behavior, for example, watching TV at your desk is probably not acceptable.
- There is more than one person in most companies, so you are able to specialize in a certain area. There are executives, managers, and individual contributors, and each has a role. Plus there are all the various functions within the business: sales, marketing, operations, human resources, finance, product development, and legal. You don't have to do it all or know it all.
- There probably is not a fully stocked kitchen near your desk, filled with snacks and drinks.
- There are no piles of dirty laundry, children fighting, whining dogs, or unpaid bills to distract you.

As you can see, your previous job provided many structures that helped you retain focus on your work and establish boundaries between your work life and your home life. You may not have recognized these structures and their benefits until now, when they are gone.

Humans are a structured species. We have structured societies, structured businesses, structured social situations (such as dating and marriage), structured activities — we like structure! Or, perhaps more accurately, we feel more comfortable in situations where there is some amount of structure.

So what's my point? Just this: if you are feeling somewhat uneasy, a little fearful, or a bit panicked at the idea of being self-employed and being your own boss — that's a natural, normal feeling! There are several potential causes for these feelings (for example, fear of failure or financial concerns), but a big portion could be due to a lack of a work-related structure.

The good news is that you can easily create your own work structure. Now that you recognize what job structure involves, it's not difficult to develop a structure tailored to your needs, goals, priorities, and preferences. Hopefully you also recognize the value that structure has in your work life. Without some structure, you will have a difficult time maintaining focus and accomplishing your goals. The structure you develop will be a key factor in your business success.

An important structure to start building right away is your support structure. Being self-employed and home-based can feel isolated, and the potential loneliness is one reason for business failure. Humans are a social species, and this challenge may make it harder to stay focused and enjoy the coaching life. Establish a network of friends and colleagues with whom you can share successes and provide support. Join your local chapter of the International Coach Federation or Coachville. Or, join the virtual ICF chapter which has regular teleconferences. In addition to your social network, consider creating an informal Board of Directors consisting of colleagues and friends who will act as sounding boards and who will motivate and energize you when you are feeling stuck or disappointed, need inspiration, or facing a major decision.

The remainder of this chapter is devoted to establishing your work structure and providing tips on improving your efficiency within that structure.

Work Schedule

The ability to choose your days and hours of work is one of the biggest benefits of being self-employed. It is recommended that you develop a rough idea of the days and hours you plan to work. This schedule, even though it's flexible, will provide you with clearer boundaries between your work and personal life. Although some people say they "work all the time" this isn't really possible or healthy!

Hours Per Week

How many hours a week do you want to work on your coaching business? This amount of time needs to include coaching appointments as well as time for sample sessions, marketing activities, business finances, professional development (i.e., training), administrative tasks, and other business related activities.

Total up the number of hours needed for your coaching appointments (a best practice is to plan 45 minutes for each 30 minute session to allow for any notes, follow-up work, and bio breaks), and then add at least four to ten hours a week for the other overhead tasks. (The term "overhead" means that the activity does not directly produce income).

You will find that the hours you spend in overhead activities will vary greatly depending on the stability of your company, the number of new clients you want to enroll, and your chosen marketing activities. You might be surprised how quickly eight hours disappear when you are working on a brochure or developing materials for a workshop.

Weekly Schedule

Once you know how many hours a week you want to work, the next step is to determine, in general, how to spread those hours across the weekdays. Here are some examples:

- Work only specific days of the week, such as Monday, Wednesday, and Friday
- Work only those hours that you function at your peak, such as from 8am to 1pm (if you are a morning person)
- Work the days and hours that your clients request, which

may include evening or weekend hours. If you choose this option, also look at what days/hours you want to do overhead activities.

- Work the days and hours that best fit with your other activities and priorities, such as the hours that your children are in daycare, or days that your spouse or significant other is at work.

Other Structures

Once you've determined your basic weekly schedule, your focus can shift to other aspects of the work structure. Here are some additional questions:

- How will you dress for work?
- When will you break for lunch?
- Will you have breaks during the day? If so, how many and when?
- What interruptions or distractions will you allow in your workday? Examples might include turning on the TV, doing household chores, walking the dog, or personal phone calls. Will there be a time limit on these events?
- Will you snack during your work time?
- Under what circumstances will you take off a morning, afternoon, or day?

Time Management

Within the hours that you work, how will you manage your time? How will you know what to work on first? Determining the answers to these questions is the goal of time management. The model presented here has seven elements: goals, tasks, priorities, task groupings, scheduling, execution, and evaluation.

Goals

The starting point for effectively managing your time is to clearly define your goals. You've already developed a business plan in Chapter Four and marketing goals in Chapter Eleven. Review those documents and select four to six goals that you want to accomplish in the next six months.

Tasks

Reaching a goal requires the right mental attitude and a set of specific tasks or activities. A goal with no action plan is just a dream; it's the actions that move you toward that goal.

In Chapter Eleven, you created a short-term marketing action plan. Perhaps one of your goals is to enroll 10 new clients into your practice within the next six months. Here are a few action steps you might choose to reach that goal:

- Once a day, visualize the practice with 10 more clients.
- Attend at least one networking event each week. Meet three new people at each event and follow up with each of them after the event.
- Offer sample sessions to five new people each week.
- Develop and send out a letter and brochure to friends, colleagues, and family members. Ask for referrals and offer sample sessions.

You might have more tasks listed to support your goal. The ones listed above are just examples. Do some brainstorming to develop a list of all the tasks possible to reach each of your goals. Break the tasks into actionable steps. For example, the last task above — sending out a letter and brochure to your network — might include actionable steps such as:

- Review notes in Chapter 13 (Marketing Materials)
- Create outline and draft of letter
- Have Karin review draft for feedback and editing

- Update address list, print off address labels
- Go to Post Office for stamps
- Print letter on letterhead and stuff envelopes

You want each of the tasks to be detailed enough that they are actionable and measurable. At the completion of this step, you will have a list of four to six goals, and each of those goals will have a list of supporting activities. Don't worry if your lists look intimidating. The next step in the process will structure the lists so that they are manageable.

Priorities

You now have several lists, each containing multiple tasks. Don't panic — you don't need to complete these tasks all at once! In fact, the goal of this step is to determine which tasks are the most important.

First, review your goals and rank them in order of importance. Next, look at the tasks associated with your highest priority goal. Which of those tasks will provide you with the greatest benefit or progress towards your goal? Mark your task list with a priority ranking. The workbook contains examples to walk you through this process. There are a few reasons why a task might be classified as high priority:

- It has a big benefit in relation to the amount of time and effort it takes.
- It is a prerequisite for some other task.
- It is a task that is fundamental to achieving your goal.

Here are a few reasons why a task might be lower on the list:

- It takes a substantial period of time to complete and has only a tangential relationship to your goal.
- It is dependent on another task that isn't complete.
- It takes a substantial period of time to complete, and

may have limited results or results that may not come about in the near term. These tasks are ones to get started on, but they should have a longer timeframe for completion.

Grouping

Determine which higher priority tasks (across *all* your goals) you want to complete in the next two months. Highlight these tasks; they now represent your To-Do list for the next two months. Post this list in a visible place in your office to remind yourself of your desired achievements for the month.

Within this list, group similar tasks, e.g., the phone calls, the purchases at the local office supply store, the networking events. To increase efficiency, do these tasks in groups. For example, it's better to make three phone calls at one time rather than at different times.

Schedule the Time

Review your generic weekly schedule and set aside blocks of time to complete these groups of tasks. For example, you may decide that you will run errands on Wednesday afternoons and make phone calls on Thursday mornings.

This schedule isn't meant to be rigid but rather a guideline for the week's events and tasks. The workbook contains some example schedules. Post your generic schedule in your office as a reminder. Following this generic schedule will allow you develop a routine, which in turn will increase your efficiency. How?

- By setting the expectation that you will work on specific types of tasks on certain days and times
- By allowing you to schedule unplanned events in a timeframe where they will have the least impact
- By giving you a tool by which you can set expectations with your family and friends (and yourself) regarding when you are working and when you are accessible

Execute with Flexibility

Each day, using your generic schedule and your prioritized task list, develop a daily to-do list. These are the specific tasks that you want to accomplish today. When you complete a task, cross it off your task list, and celebrate! If you don't finish a task, mark it as your first priority for the next time you work on that task group.

Always allow yourself some flexibility to adapt your daily schedule for emergencies, unanticipated events, or deadlines. But resume your schedule as soon as you are able.

Evaluate Your Progress

After a month's time, evaluate your progress toward your goals and also your satisfaction with your schedule and structure. Celebrate all the progress you've made! While reviewing your progress, look for trends. For example, were particular days of the week more difficult than expected? If so, determine how to rearrange your generic schedule to better accommodate the amount of work or the last minute changes you experienced. Don't criticize yourself. Instead just acknowledge what you have learned, and adjust accordingly.

Your schedule will change and adapt over time, and your knowledge of how much work you can realistically accomplish in a day, week, or month will increase as you continue to use the system, review your progress, notice what you have learned, and make adjustments.

You have now created several documents that will facilitate your progress towards your goals: goal list, prioritized task list, monthly task list, generic weekly schedule, and daily to-do list.

There are products available that can help you keep track of your goals, tasks, priorities, and to-do lists. Some of the products are paper-based (e.g., calendars, planners, pads of paper) and some are computer-based (e.g., PDAs and time management software).

Increasing Efficiency

There is no downside to being more efficient. It saves you time and effort, and because you are more productive you have more time to pursue other activities or interests.

Unfortunately, there is no single way to maximize efficiency. Instead, there are many small habits or behaviors that, when combined, can impact your productivity. Here are some tips to increase your overall efficiency:

- Get a coach! Having a good coach will greatly increase your efficiency and keep you focused.
- Multi-task, meaning do more than one thing at a time. If you are watching TV, flip through your business magazines and rip out interesting articles for later review, or listen to a book on tape while exercising.
- When reading periodicals, start with the table of contents and look at only the interesting articles. If nothing catches your eye in the table of contents, toss it out.
- Use email when a phone call isn't necessary. Email can increase efficiency by allowing for short messages without a potentially lengthier phone conversation.
- Learn to say no to those requests that are not high priority or that do not move you toward your goals. This is a hard habit to develop, but it gets easier with practice.
- Use idle time for small tasks that can be accomplished quickly. For example, order office supplies over the Internet while you are on hold on the phone. File a stack of papers if you find yourself with a few extra minutes before your next coaching session. Keep a stack of unread articles close at hand to read while you are waiting for a call. When you encounter a quick task, set it aside until there is a short downtime to fill in.
- Take several short breaks during the day to clear your mind and move your muscles, such as getting the mail or walking around the block. Short breaks will increase

your mental clarity and efficiency.

- Use your support structure to avoid loneliness.
- Screen your phone calls. Minimizing the number of interruptions will increase your productivity.
- Build a time cushion into your daily plans. If you think a task with take three hours, plan for four hours. This allows you time for the unanticipated delays.
- Don't sweat the small decisions. The amount of time and energy you spend on a decision should be in proportion to the size of the decision's consequence. For those decisions that are of little consequence, go with your gut feeling or a quick decision.
- Develop a routine for each time you need to "go to work." Examples include an alarm clock going off, going for a brisk walk with the dog, or the end of a morning news program. Each of these could be a signal to go to work. The same holds true at night when you complete your work. Your last tasks might be to check your voicemail, organize your desk, turn off your computer, and then close the door to your office. The routine will help you change gears from your work life to your home life.
- Use a Do Not Disturb sign on your office door and set the expectation with your family that you are not to be disturbed when the sign is posted.
- Designate a separate space in the house as your office. Talk with your family about your need for quiet when you are in that space. Keep the space as free from personal belongings as possible.
- Hire someone to do things that are easily delegated and/ or at which you are not skilled. Examples include hiring an accountant to do your bookkeeping and taxes, or a web developer to design your web site.

Addressing Procrastination

You're probably familiar with the situation: you have a task to do and you can't make any progress on it. It seems much easier to put the task off to another day when you hope you will feel more motivated.

There are several potential causes for procrastination and recognizing the underlying reason for the delay may help you to break the cycle. Listed here are some tips to address and combat the most common causes.

Large, Overwhelming Tasks

Where to start? The task seems so big, how can I succeed? The answer is to break the huge task into multiple, smaller, manageable steps that each take no more than an hour to complete. The first step is to make the list of the smaller steps, and then continue from there.

Fear

One of the major causes of procrastination is fear of something — success, failure, change, or loss. Here are two alternatives to address and conquer your fears:

- Ask yourself "What about this task makes me afraid?" Write down all your answers, then look at each one. Is the fear realistic? If not, physically cross it off the page and tell yourself "This is an unrealistic fear." If the fear is realistic, think through how you would handle the situation if it occurs. By acknowledging your fears, getting them on paper, and looking at each one, you will free yourself from their power.
- Spend time reviewing your business vision and goals. By remembering your "bigger game," your motivation and enthusiasm will be rekindled and help you to work through your fear.

"As Soon As" Syndrome

"I'll go to a networking event *as soon as* my brochure is done" or "I'll offer sample sessions *as soon as* my intake packet is complete." This is a trap. You don't need to have a brochure to network, and you don't need an intake packet to offer sample sessions. Get out of the trap by doing it now. Don't wait!

An Unpleasant Task

One example that most people can relate to is filing taxes. Many people are standing in line at the post office at 11:59pm on April 15th. Here are a couple of options to tackle an unpleasant task:

- Visualize how good you will feel when the task is done.
- Promise yourself a reward when it is done. Break the task into smaller segments, each with its own reward.
- Do the task first thing in the day. Then you will feel good all afternoon and evening.
- Hire someone to do it for you.

Perfectionism

Recognize that nothing is perfect. There is no such thing as the perfect brochure or the perfect web site. Before you start the task, define for yourself what "good enough" would look like and aim for that. Set specific goals and deadlines.

16

Business Contact Information

In business for yourself, not by yourself.

RAY KROC

IT'S HARD TO IMAGINE that fewer than ten years ago, small businesses could manage with just a phone number and a street address. Today, there is a multitude of contact methods and each has several alternatives to review before you can make an educated choice. In this chapter, I'll provide some details that will hopefully make your decision process a little easier and better informed. Specifically, the following contact methods will be discussed:

- Street Address
- Business Phone
- Fax Number
- Internet Access and Service Providers
- Types of Internet Connections
- Email Accounts
- Domain Names and Web Hosting

Street Address

Options for your mailing/street address are related to the options for where you physically perform your coaching services. Alternatives include:

- Your home address
- A P.O. box at your local post office
- A box at your local mail receiving service center, such as Mail Boxes Etc. or Postal Express.
- If you do in-person coaching and rent or lease office space, you could use that address. Private practice therapists or psychiatrists may have an extra office to rent, or may rent out their office on specific days of the week.
- A higher-cost alternative is a "serviced" office complex, where you rent your own small office. Many of these office complexes offer administrative support and other services along with the office space. This type of arrangement is typically available only in larger cities.

Business Phone

- Since the majority of your coaching work will be by phone, you will need a good quality telephone and a headset (more information in Chapter Seventeen).
- Voice mail, or a good quality answering machine, is a requirement for your business, and helps project a professional image. Using voice mail is preferable to an answering machine as it sounds more professional, has better sound quality, and it's also easier to retrieve, store, and review your messages.
- A separate business phone line will also enhance your professional image. However, when you first start out, you may not have the cash flow to cover the extra expense. If this is the case, the outgoing message on your

answering machine or voice mail should say something like "You've reached the home of Chris and Dorcas and the office of Clarity in Action Coaching." In addition, if you use an answering machine, use one mailbox for personal messages and another for business messages.

- A business line is billed at a higher monthly and per-minute rate than a residential line, but is necessary if you want to list the number using your business name and/or have a listing in the Yellow Pages. You may be required to get a new phone number if you later want to switch the line to a residential listing.

- Do you want a toll-free number? This depends on the number and location of your clients, your cash flow and your marketing strategy. If you have relatively few clients or if most of them are in your local area, then a toll-free number may represent an extra expense with little benefit. However, if you have many clients who call you long distance, or if you want to have a toll-free number as a competitive advantage, then the additional expense might be justified. International toll-free numbers are also available if you have clients in other countries.

- Do some research on the various long distance carriers. The rates vary tremendously across companies! What carrier is best for you depends on your calling patterns, for example, are most of your calls in-state (intrastate) or between states (interstate)? The same recommendation — research multiple carriers — holds true for mobile phones as well.

- There are alternatives that allow you to turn your PC into a phone and make phone calls via the Internet. This is a relatively new technology, and may not be ready for professional use yet. However, these services are worth mentioning here as technologies to watch for future developments. Two companies that provide PC-to-phone and PC-to-PC phone services are: PhoneFree.com, and Net2Phone.com.

Fax Number

- You may not need a fax number, but if you do, one option is to have your business phone and fax machine share one phone number. This option doesn't look very professional, but if you receive few faxes it may not be worth the effort and cost to set up a separate number. However, there are a few drawbacks to having only one phone number for your phone and fax:
  - You can't use voice mail with this arrangement, so you will need to have a good quality answering machine.
  - In your outgoing message on your answering machine, you will need to tell the caller when to send the fax ("If you are sending a fax, press Start now"), or you will need a small electronic box (typically known as a telephone line sharing device) that can automatically detect the fax signal and route the call to the fax machine. These boxes can typically be purchased at an office supply store or from electronics mail order sources. They can be relatively inexpensive and easy to set up, but have been known to be slightly inconsistent in their functioning due to variations in the telephone signal strength of the incoming call.
  - In some locations you are able to use phone company voicemail along with a telephone line-sharing device. Read your telephone line sharing device documentation to see if your equipment will support this configuration.
- An option for practices that receive many faxes, or that want a more professional appearance, is to have a separate number for the fax machine.
- If you have a dial-up ISDN line (further described in a later section), you can use one of the ISDN numbers for the fax machine. This provides a separate line and phone number for the fax machine, but also allows the ISDN

connection to use that line when no fax is being transmitted or received.

- If you don't mind receiving your faxes via email, there are Internet based services that will receive your faxes and send them to you as email attachments. Some of these services can also handle your voicemail messages the same way. Two of these services are jfax.com and efax.com.

Internet Access

As a small business owner, you will find that your use of the Internet (including email) will increase as your business grows. The Internet can be a great productivity enhancer and marketing tool. Having a web site for your practice is an excellent marketing tool, both to get "click through" traffic (when users find your site through a search engine or a linked web site) and to act as an online brochure for your practice. Web sites are discussed further in Chapter Thirteen.

Email (an aspect of the Internet) allows easy communication with colleagues and clients. It improves your productivity by allowing you to send concise, focused messages at practically any time of the day or night. You can also read the replies at any time as well. In contrast, when communicating by phone, you either need to leave a message (and hope you're around for the return call) or engage in a conversation that may last longer than necessary. This is not to say that phone conversations are bad, just that they can be less efficient.

Email can also be used as a business asset and marketing tool to help you develop a strong support network, share best practices, and contact potential clients. As your company grows, you will want to make sure that you check your email on a daily basis.

Although you may already have email and Internet access, you should examine your current Internet configuration (equipment and services) to ensure that the process you use is streamlined and easy to use. If the process or programs you use are confusing, cumbersome, or time consuming, the chances that you will fully utilize the advantages of the Internet diminish.

There are four main elements involved in the access and use of the Internet and your email account. These elements will be discussed in the following sections.

1. An Internet Service Provider (ISP) physically connects your computer to the Internet through software and physical equipment
2. The physical equipment you use to connect your computer to the Internet Service Provider (e.g., analog modem, DSL, ISDN)
3. An email service provider sets up and manages your email account
4. A web hosting service provider sets up and manages your web site

Many larger Internet-related companies may provide several of the elements listed above. For example, AOL is an Internet Service Provider (i.e., connects your PC to the Internet), an email service provider, and a web hosting service provider. Other companies may offer just one of the services. Yahoo! offers another unique example. Yahoo! started out as a directory to web sites, then added Internet search engine features. Currently, Yahoo! also provides free email accounts and partners with other companies to offer Internet access.

The objective here is not to confuse you, but rather to point out that it is difficult to do an apples-to-apples comparison across Internet-related companies due to the many variations and combinations of service offerings. When you look into these types of companies, make sure you understand which components or services are being offered.

Internet Service Providers

Accessing the Internet from your computer requires the services of an Internet Service Provider (ISP). An ISP will provide you with the connection between your computer and the Internet. There are several decision criteria to consider when selecting an ISP.

- An ISP might be a local company (look in the Yellow Pages under Internet Access) or a nationwide provider such as Earthlink, Microsoft Network, or America Online. Local ISPs typically have the advantages of ease of contact and lower cost. However, disadvantages may include variable service quality and only a local access number (an issue for travelers who need remote access to the Internet). The nationwide providers will have more consistent service, but may not have local access numbers in all geographic locations, and may provide lower quality customer service and additional constraints.
- Your choice of connection method (discussed in the following section) may narrow your ISP options.

Types of Internet Connections

Currently, there are six Internet access equipment options most suitable to small businesses. A summary table of these options is located in the workbook.

- Analog Modem
- ISDN
- Cable
- DSL
- Satellite
- Wireless

These options can be compared on a few key features: cost, availability of ISPs that support the technology, speed of download (getting information from the Internet) and upload (sending back your requests or information to the Internet), and equipment requirements.

In addition, another distinction is between dial-up Internet connections vs. full-time connections. Having a dial-up account means that you dial into the ISP only when you need Internet access (for example to send mail, receive mail, or visit a web site). In contrast, with a full-time connection, you are always linked to the ISP and the Internet, whenever your computer is on. In general, full-time connections are more expensive than dial-ups but may be more convenient. In addition, there are security concerns with a full-time connection as the connection could more easily allow hackers to access your computer. Therefore a full-time connection typically has some enhanced security features and considerations.

Analog Modem

- Analog modems represent the oldest technology. These modems can be either internal or external to your computer. They are currently the most common type of Internet access device and also the slowest. However, this option does give you the largest choice of ISPs.
- Most ISPs can accept hookups with 56k modems (also known as V90 modems). The maximum theoretical download speed is 56kbps; the upload speed is limited to about 30kbps.
- This type of connection uses a regular telephone line, and a few companies offer an "Internet caller ID" feature so that you can find out who is calling without breaking the Internet connection.
- Most analog modems are used with dial-up accounts, but full-time accounts are available, though relatively expensive.
- Analog modems are portable so you can take them on

business trips (along with your laptop computer), whereas the other options are not portable.

- Important note: When using an analog modem in a hotel, you must make sure that the phone line is not digital. Hooking an analog modem to a digital line won't work and may damage your modem. You can easily check the phone line with a Digital Phone Line Tester. Some larger hotels provide specific data ports on their telephones. If they don't, you may be able to unplug the phone and plug the telephone line directly into the modem. But test the line before you plug it in!

ISDN

- This option represents a step up in speed, complexity, and cost from an analog modem. ISDN service requires a special ISDN phone line to be installed.
- ISDN service is not available everywhere. Check with your local phone company. In addition, not all ISPs can support ISDN access.
- The upload and download speeds aren't much faster than an analog modem (approx. 64kbps for one channel, 128kbps for two channels).
- The ISDN line consists of two channels; each channel can transmit data at up to 64kbps. There are three ways that the channels can be set up.
  1. You could have two phone numbers for the one ISDN line, one number for each channel. Each channel can be used independently for either voice or data. This way you can be talking on one channel or receiving a fax, and the other channel can be used for Internet access. Or you can use both channels together for faster Internet access. This option would be a dial-up service, meaning that you would call up the service only when you need access to the Internet. A disadvantage to this option is that some phone companies will have metering charges dur-

ing certain times of the day, so high usage could make this option more expensive.

2. You could have only one phone number for the ISDN line and both channels are used only for Internet access with a consistent speed of 128kbps. The disadvantage is that no voice or fax communication is possible. The advantage is usually that there are no per-minute charges.

3. A third alternative is a full-time ISDN connection. This is similar to the second option in that the line could not be used for phone or fax, but the connection is full-time and the cost is usually much higher. Similar to the full-time analog modem connection, there are security issues to consider.

Cable

- This option uses your television cable line to connect to the Internet. Call your local cable company to see if it is offered in your area.
- Your choice of ISP will be limited. In some cases you may have to use the ISP selected by your cable company.
- This type of connection has the potential for substantially faster upload and download speeds than ISDN. How much faster depends on the cable company and on the number of neighbors using their cable modems at the same time. It is possible to have 10MBs download speed (roughly 100 times the ISDN speed), although speeds of about 10 times ISDN are more typical. The upload speed also depends on the cable company. Upload and download speeds will be affected by how many people in your neighborhood are accessing the Internet via cable at the same time.
- This type of connection is full-time and once again there are security considerations.

DSL

- This option uses a standard telephone line, but is setup so that you can use the phone for voice communication while simultaneously accessing the Internet.
- Upload and download speeds are somewhat comparable to cable. Depending on the phone company, the specific service, and the ISP, uploads are generally slower than downloads. Typical speeds might be 384kbps (three times ISDN) upload and 768kbps download (six times ISDN).
- DSL uses a full-time connection and once again there are security considerations.

Satellite

- This option uses a small satellite dish similar to the TV satellite dishes, and may include TV satellite functionality.
- The upload and download speeds can be up to 400kbps (greater than three times ISDN).
- This equipment option is currently not widely used but is gaining popularity, especially in areas that have limited cable and phone services.
- Currently, there are only two sources for satellite equipment. The industry leader is DirecWay, and a relatively new company is StarBand Communications.

Wireless

- This option uses wireless technology to provide connection speeds similar to DSL. It is gaining popularity especially in areas that have limited cable and phone services. However, service areas are limited so call your local ISP to see if it is offered in your area. In addition, not all ISPs can support wireless access.
- After a site visit, the ISP would install a small antenna on your residence (or business location). In addition,

you would need specific wireless hardware within your
computer.
- Wireless uses a full-time connection and there are security considerations.

The workbook contains a table that compares the various
Internet access methods on some key features.

Email Accounts

Email has become a standard communication method in the
business world. There are basically three alternatives to determine how you will get your email.

1. Your ISP may also be an email service provider and may
   include at least one free mailbox; some ISPs will also
   give you a small of amount of web space.
2. There are also free email accounts available from
   yahoo.com, hotmail.com and others. These email accounts generally are web based, meaning that you can
   access them using a web browser instead of a separate
   email program.
3. A third alternative is to purchase your own domain
   name, which is discussed in the following section.

These alternatives vary in price, professional appearance,
and ease of setup. Option #1 is a minimum requirement.
Option #2 cannot stand on its own but must be done in con-
junction with having an ISP to access your email account.
Option #3 is the most expensive, most professional looking,
and the most complex to set up.

Regardless of how you get your email, remember to maintain a professional image when choosing your email name.
Use your business name or an easy to remember abbreviation of it. Avoid cute, trendy, or overly personal email names.

Domain Names

The purpose of a domain name is to provide your business with a unique Internet address. If you plan to have a web site, or unique email address, then you will need to research and purchase (also known as registering, but not to be confused with search engine registration discussed in Chapter Thirteen) a domain name. This annual purchase will give you the right to use the domain name. In addition, you will need to hire the services of a web hosting company to host or store your domain name and your web site.

Using your own domain name gives your business a more professional appearance. You can use your domain name just for email, or you can create web site to describe your practice (discussed in Chapter Thirteen). There are many Internet-based companies that act as domain name registrars. The process to register a domain name is very simple, and the cost to purchase a domain name is as low as $9 per year.

In some cases, people will just purchase the domain name but not use it right away. This is called "parking" the domain name. The purchaser has secured the rights to use the domain name, but for right now the name is not in active use. Parking a domain name can be done by either the domain name registration company or by some web hosting companies. It is typically a free service or very nominal charge. The advantage of registering a domain name and parking it is that you are assured of the rights to use the name.

Web Hosting

To use your registered domain name, you need to hire the services of a web hosting company. This company will provide the physical location and supporting services for your email account and/or web site. Your web host does not need to be local to you.

There are a multitude of web hosting companies, with a wide variety of features, services, and costs. Here are three alternative scenarios to help you narrow your choices.

1. Does your ISP offer web hosting services? If so, you can enjoy one-stop shopping.
2. Use a separate company for your web hosting services. There are several web sites that publish rankings of the top web hosting companies.
3. Use web forwarding from a web host to your ISP. Does your ISP provide you with a web address as described in the previous section (www.your-isp.com/~your-id)? If yes, you could forward any web activity and/or email from your domain name to your ISP site. Although you would still need to hire a web host, the only feature you would need would be web forwarding.

Regardless of which scenario you choose, you will need to look at the features and services of the web hosting companies. Chapter Sixteen in the workbook has a table of key features to compare.

Web hosting companies will provide you with email addresses along with web site hosting. With your own domain name, your email ID can be your personal name (or abbreviation), since the domain name identifies your business, such as your-name@your-domain-name.com. You may also want to set up an email account of info@your-domain-name.com for use on your web page, brochures, and other marketing materials.

You will continue to need your ISP service to provide you the connection between your computer and the Internet, so don't cancel that service! Before you select your web host and/or ISP, verify that the two companies and technologies will work with each other, i.e., that you are able to retrieve your email from your web host location.

17

Designing
Your Office

*You are a product of your environment.
So choose the environment that will best develop
you toward your objective. Analyze your life in terms
of its environment. Are the things around you
helping you toward success — or are they holding
you back?*

CLEMENT STONE

ONE OF THE GREAT FEATURES of a coaching business is that it requires relatively little to start: a telephone, some paper, and some privacy is the minimum required. Regardless of whether your "office" is located at your kitchen table, in its own room, or in a downtown building, you need to pay attention to your work environment to make it pleasant, comfortable, and efficient. Some additional pieces of equipment and processes will increase your productivity and make your worklife less stressful.

Managing the Paperwork

The wave of information that comes at us each day is astounding. It's easy to get overwhelmed with the amount of paper mail, email, and voice mails we receive, let alone the information we get off the Internet. To make matters more complicated, we deal with information in both paper and electronic form. The futurists' vision of a paperless office is still a long way off. Until that day arrives, we will continue to have stacks of paper to retain and manage.

Where to put it all? Later, when the information is needed, where did it go? These frustrating questions are often to blame for interruptions in our workflow and lost opportunities. The inability to find needed information is probably the single most common form of home office inefficiency. If you ever hear yourself say "I know it's here but I'll have to look for it," that's a sign that your current filing system isn't working well.

Regardless of the size of your business, it's helpful to have a system for processing and organizing the information that crosses your desk. This includes coaching information (such as client files), your financial and legal information (including budgets, receipts, tax forms, account statements), and marketing materials (such as brochures, networking dates, business cards received, mailing lists).

The primary purpose for a filing and organizing system is the *retrieval* of information, not the storage. Your system needs to be simple, easy-to-use, and compact. It also needs to be flexible so you can add or discard items as needed.

The system presented here is based on a mnemonic device you may have learned in a high school English class, the five Ws: who, what, where, when, and why. However, this model uses a slightly different order: who, why, what, where, and when. Each of the following sections builds upon the previous ones with the end result being a well-organized, efficient, and stress-reducing system.

The first item is pretty straightforward: Who? Unless you have an administrative assistant, the "who" will be you. Enough said.

Why Keep It

With each item that you encounter (paper or electronic), ask yourself: Why would I need to keep this? Does the information have some value — a document I need to retain, notes that I will refer to, an article to copy for handouts?

Your first step in getting organized is to throw out all the items you don't need. Don't try to organize the stuff you're keeping; that will be the next step. In this first step, just go through your piles and stacks and boxes of paper and clean out all the documents and items that do not provide value to you or your business.

If the item has no value then toss it in the recycle bin! Don't even open those pieces of junk mail and junk email. Be aggressive about throwing things out. A rule of thumb is: if you haven't used something in the past year, and it has no sentimental or monetary or legal value, but "it might come in handy someday," then it should be tossed out. (Specific record retention guidelines for legal and financial information are provided in the workbook.) If there is a magazine with an interesting article, cut out the article and recycle the rest. You will feel much less cluttered and very productive by just clearing out all the unneeded items. When in doubt about keeping something, ask yourself the following questions:

- What will I use it for?
- Under what circumstances might I need it?
- What would happen if I didn't have it?

What Type of Information

Each piece of information has one of four distinct purposes:

1. Current information that is time sensitive
2. Reference materials and resources
3. Masters that are used for duplication
4. Archive information that contains historical data

All four types of information need to be accessible, but can vary on their ease of access. For example, your current information on client billings needs to be at your fingertips, but your tax return from last year can probably be stored in the attic.

In addition, the information can be classified into different categories, with various topics within each category. The workbook contains some example categories, topics, and their purposes.

Where to Store It

"Ease of access" can be translated into the physical location of the information. You should establish four standard storage locations so the information will not be scattered around:

1. At your desk (hard copy or on your computer)
2. At your reading location (e.g., couch, reading chair)
3. In the general vicinity of your office (e.g., farther from your desk or in another room)
4. An archive storage area (e.g., attic, file cabinet), which can be distant from your office.

At Your Desk might be storage locations such as a standing file holder, a small file cabinet, and a computer. All the hard copy "current" files should be placed so that they are literally at your fingertips. Provided in the workbook are some helpful techniques to organize this storage location.

At Your Reading Location would be the unread magazines, books, journals, and other reading materials. In addition, you should have three bins nearby for material to recycle, file, or donate. Once you have read an item, it should be either kept for reference, given away, or recycled.

Locations In The General Vicinity of your office would include all the reference materials and masters. These can be stored in a bookcase or file cabinet located near your office. These documents are for occasional review and/or duplication. It is recommended that you group your reference material by category and topic to make it easier to locate a specific item.

Archive Information, which is seldom reviewed, can be located quite far from your office, such as at the other end of the house, in a box in the back of a closet, in the attic, or in a local storage locker. Each box should be clearly labeled with the contents as well as with the storage date and the future disposal date.

When to Process It

Most filing systems, no matter how informal, involve these same tasks. So what makes this system work better? The answer is the addition of *timing* and *a process*. Other filing systems are often missing the *"when"* of filing — having a regular time with an established routine for handing and filing the information.

By having a regular routine established for processing documents and information, you will get into the habit of processing information, filing, and being organized. The key is to choose particular days of the week, month, quarter, and year to perform certain tasks and then mark those days on your calendar.

For example, the end of the first week of each month is a good time to enter and file any expense receipts from the previous month, payments you've received from clients, and fill out your bank deposit slip. At the same time you could update your budget with the actual expenses and income figures for the previous month. In Chapter Eight it was suggested that you do your invoicing at the end of the third week. On the same day you could also review your progress toward your business goals, as described in Chapter Fifteen.

The most critical element is to develop a habit of doing

these tasks, so that you do them automatically. To make the tasks seem less burdensome, provide an incentive. While paying the bills, why not watch a favorite movie? Filing might become more enjoyable while you are listening to music or watching Oprah. Treat yourself to a nice evening out after you've completed your monthly accounting tasks. You probably have other motivational tips that you use with your coaching clients. Use them with yourself!

In the workbook is an example calendar for a year's worth of paper and information processing and management. This table is just an example; feel free to establish your own calendar.

Record Retention

Some records should be retained for a specific period of time, such as tax forms and specific financial and legal transactions. When you move these records into an archive location or box (at the end of the year in which the transaction took place), write the storage date and the future disposal date on the outside of the file or box. That will simplify your annual cleanup task. Listed in the workbook are some guidelines for the length of time that specific documents should be retained. Ask your accountant or lawyer for additional guidance, if needed.

Office Equipment

When you first start out, the only office equipment you must have is a phone. But as your business grows, you might want to add equipment to increase your productivity and enhance your professional appearance. Each of the items listed here will be discussed, including desirable features to look for during your selection process.

- Telephone and headset
- Answering machine or voicemail
- Personal computer (Windows or Mac)
- Printer and fax machine
- Office furniture

Telephone and Headset

Look for a telephone that has the following features:

- Two-line phone (if you have a separate business line)
- Cordless (great for moving around while coaching)
- Headset jack
- Mute button
- Adjustable ring volume
- Redial and automatic redial
- Hold and call-on-hold indicator
- Speed dial or programmable memory keys
- Caller ID display
- Conferencing or three-way calling ability

Headsets are a must-have for coaches! A headset lets you be more productive and is also easier on your upper body. With your hands free you'll be able to take notes, reach for files, look up information, and have greater mobility. In addition, your body will be more comfortable and relaxed.

Headsets are a fairly specialized item that aren't available at many retail stores. What type of headset you can use will depend on what brand and model of phone you have. There are many styles to choose from — corded and cordless, using a headset jack or an amplifier, single ear or double ear, with or without mute button. If you have questions, the customer service personnel at your chosen company should be able to assist you. Some recommended companies are listed in the workbook.

Messaging

Voice mail is typically acquired through your local phone company or through your mobile phone service company. Voice mail is recommended over an answering machine for the following reasons:

- Projects a more professional image due to better sound quality and greater options for the caller (such as greeting bypass, message review and re-record, and marking the message as urgent)
- Removes the worry about power outages erasing your outgoing and incoming messages
- Typically easier to access remotely

If you are unable to get voice mail, or prefer to use an answering machine, look for a machine that has the following features:

- Reliable performance and battery back-up
- Good sound quality (i.e., not tinny)
- Variable-length incoming message so the caller doesn't get cut off (voice activated or VOX setting)
- Ring selector (lets you set the number of rings before the machine answers). One of the options should be a "toll saver" option so that the phone will pick up after one ring if there are messages waiting, and won't pick up until after four rings if there are no messages. This saves you money when you call in to pick up your messages.
- 30 minutes or greater total record time
- Lets the caller know if the machine is full (otherwise the call just goes unanswered)
- Able to skip and store messages
- Easy remote access for message retrieval
- Call counter plus date and time stamp on each message
- Obvious, easy-to-use controls

Office Computer

Personal computers are becoming faster, less expensive, and smaller. These are all positive trends. However, many of the recent technology advances are overkill for a small business or a typical home user. So what's the reason for pointing this out? Just this: if you are an average personal computer user, you do not need the latest and greatest in personal computer technology! The most cost-effective option is to look for a good deal on last year's model — really! If you feel compelled to buy the latest and the greatest, that's fine. But know that you are paying more than necessary and buying more computer than you probably need.

Another option to reduce cost is to look for refurbished models. These are computers that came back to the factory for some problem, were fixed, tested, and are now available for sale. Refurbished models can be substantially less expensive than new models. But they may come with a shorter warranty period, which increases your risk as a consumer.

Printers and Fax Machine

The two most common types of printers on the market use either laser or ink-jet technology, and both can do either black-only or color printing. An increasingly popular option for small businesses is the multi-function printer, which acts as a printer, fax machine, copier, and scanner. These machines use either color ink-jet or laser technology.

Office Ergonomics

Being self-employed brings both freedom and responsibility in the running of your business, the scheduling of your workdays, and the setup of your office. But if your work gives you aches, pains, or even a disabling syndrome, you're the one who will pay for it — literally.

The goal of ergonomics is to design a workspace that is both comfortable and safe. Invest a little time to learn about ergonomics and then put that knowledge to use. Remember: prevention is much less expensive than disability. Here are a few guidelines that will help protect you, even if your desk is the kitchen table.

- If you have only one splurge for your office, it should be a good chair. Your office chair is one of the most important elements in maintaining your physical health. Take time to find one that fits you well and is comfortable. Prices can range up to $1,500 but good chairs can be found in the $200 to $400 range. The chair should be as adjustable as possible. Typical adjustment points include:
  - Back support (up or down, tilt forward or back)
  - Lumbar support (more or less, higher or lower)
  - Arm rests (height and angle)
  - Height of seat
  - Tilt of seat (knees up or down)
  - Ability to rock back and forth in the chair

  When you sit in the chair, you should be able to adjust it so that when your feet are flat on the floor, your thighs are horizontal to the floor. The chair should provide good back support and feel comfortable in a variety of positions.
- Standard table height (29–30 inches) is too high for a comfortable work surface. Buy a real desk as soon as you can afford it, preferably one with an adjustable area for your computer and keyboard.
- Your keyboard height should be at 26-28 inches. Using wrist pads for both your keyboard and mouse will decrease wrist strain.
- Your computer monitor should be positioned so that it is directly across and slightly down from your straight-ahead field of vision. It should also be placed about 18-

25 inches from your face. Minimize the amount of glare on your monitor by placing it perpendicular to any windows or strong light sources. You may want to close any shades or curtains to further reduce glare.

- If you often refer to documents while typing, use a document holder so that you don't need to move your neck awkwardly.
- When you are seated at your computer, your body should be positioned so that:
  - There is a 90 degree angle at your elbow, with your forearms horizontal to the floor and comfortable on the keyboard
  - Your thighs are horizontal to the floor, with your feet either flat on the floor or on a foot rest
  - The monitor is directly in front of and slightly lower than your straight-ahead line of sight
- Take breaks often to stretch and change your position. Vary your work routine so you don't do one particular movement or sit in one position for an extended period of time.
- Take any persistent pain seriously and talk with your doctor about it.

These tips will increase your body's enjoyment of your work and your office. With a comfortable body, your mind will be free to focus completely on your coaching and your clients.

Index

About the Author

D ORCAS KELLEY is passionate about the success of your life and your lifework! Her vision is to transform the world of coaching, one coach at a time, by helping each one discover their power and confidence as the leader of their coaching business. She is committed not only to the success of each individual coach, but also to the long-term flourishing of the industry.

Dorcas coaches entrepreneurs, business owners, professionals, and high achievers of all kinds to reach the next level of success in their business and personal lives. In the process, her clients develop greater clarity, focus, and an increased capacity for effective action. Dorcas skillfully blends head and heart — creative intelligence along with calm compassion and humor — in all her work.

A successful entrepreneur and business owner since 1993, she is founder and president of both Kelley-Naumchik Consulting LLC, and Clarity In Action. Prior to 1993, Dorcas worked for Hewlett-Packard Company as an internal consultant and coach, and for Andersen Consulting. Drawing on her years of private and public sector expertise, she has always been a motivator of people and a model of peak performance.

Additionally, she is a popular speaker, workshop and teleclass leader, providing vibrant and content-rich presentations on a wide variety of topics, ranging from business startup and growth to coaching concepts to self-publishing.

Dorcas is a Certified Professional CoActive Coach through The Coaches Training Institute, a Certified Management Consultant through the Institute of Management Consultants, and an Associate Certified Coach through the International Coach Federation. A member of Phi Beta Kappa, her credentials also include an MBA with High Honors from UC Los Angeles and a BA with Highest Honors in Sociology from UC Santa Barbara.

Dorcas lives and thrives in the Monterey Bay area of Northern California with her husband Chris, three cats, three dogs, two goats, and a sheep named Laverne.

Do You Have Questions or Feedback?
I'd like to hear from you!

I welcome your feedback, suggestions, and questions, and I'll try to reply in a timely fashion. Your question may be selected to be answered in my free e-zine "The Business of Coaching℠ " (which you can sign up for at www.thebusinessofcoaching.com)

Please send me an email:
dorcask@clarityinaction.com

Visit our web sites:
www.thebusinessofcoaching.com
www.clarityinaction.com
www.knconsult.com

I Wish You Success
and Good Fortune
in Your Business Adventure!